The Feminist Companion to the Bible
(Second Series)

7

Editor
Athalya Brenner

Sheffield Academic Press

Samuel and Kings

A Feminist Companion to the Bible
(Second Series)

edited by Athalya Brenner

Copyright © 2000 Sheffield Academic Press

Published by Sheffield Academic Press Ltd
Mansion House
19 Kingfield Road
Sheffield, S11 9AS
England

Printed on acid-free paper in Great Britain
by The Cromwell Press
Trowbridge, Wiltshire

British Library Cataloguing in Publication Data

A catalogue record for this book is available
from the British Library

ISBN 1-84127-082-2

To the memory of

_____

Fokkelien van Dijk-Hemmes

ת·נ·צ·ב·ה·

CONTENTS

ABBREVIATIONS

AB	Anchor Bible
ANEP	James B. Pritchard (ed.), *Ancient Near East in Pictures Relating to the Old Testament* (Princeton: Princeton University Press, 1954)
ATD	Das Alte Testament Deutsch
BARev	*Biblical Archaeology Review*
BDB	Francis Brown, S.R. Driver and Charles A. Briggs, *A Hebrew and English Lexicon of the Old Testament* (Oxford: Clarendon Press, 1907)
BibInt	*Biblical Interpretation: A Journal of Contemporary Approaches*
BibRes	*Biblical Research*
BZ	*Biblische Zeitschrift*
CAD	Ignace I. Gelb *et al.* (eds.), *The Assyrian Dictionary of the Oriental Institute of the University of Chicago* (Chicago: Oriental Institute, 1964–)
CBQ	*Catholic Biblical Quarterly*
EvQ	*Evangelical Quarterly*
FOTL	The Forms of the Old Testament Literature
GKC	*Gesenius' Hebrew Grammar* (ed. E. Kautzsch, revised and trans. A.E. Cowley; Oxford: Clarendon Press, 1910)
IDB	George Arthur Buttrick (ed.), *The Interpreter's Dictionary of the Bible* (4 vols.; Nashville: Abingdon Press, 1962)
JBL	*Journal of Biblical Literature*
JNES	*Journal of Near Eastern Studies*
JSOT	*Journal for the Study of the Old Testament*
JSOTSup	*Journal for the Study of the Old Testament*, Supplement Series
KAT	Kommentar zum Alten Testament
LA	*Lexikon der Ägyptologie*
OTL	Old Testament Library
TCS	*Texts from Cuneiform Sources*
VT	*Vetus Testamentum*
VTSup	*Vetus Testamentum*, Supplements
WdF	Wege der Forschung
ZBKat	Zürcher Bibelkommentare—Altes Testament

LIST OF CONTRIBUTORS

Adrien Janis Bledstein, 5459 S Hyde Park Blvd, Chicago, IL 60615-5801, USA

Athalya Brenner, Department of Theology and Religious Studies, Faculty of the Humanities, University of Amsterdam, Oude Turfmarkt 147, 1012 GC Amsterdam, The Netherlands

Lillian R. Klein, 7108 Millwood Road, Bethesda, MD 20817-6145, USA

Laurel Lanner, Department of Theology and Religious Studies, University of Otago, PO Box 56, Dunedin, New Zealand

Uta Schmidt, Department of Old Testament, Evangelical Theology, Phillips-Universität Marburg, Lahntor 3, D-35037 Marburg, Germany

Silvia Schroer, Feldeggstr 28, CH-3098 Konizn, Switzerland

Mary E. Shields, Trinity Lutheran Seminary, 2199 E Main Street, Columbus, OH 43209, USA

Jopie Siebert-Hommes, Zuster Klijnstralaan 24, NL-7339 MC Ugchelen

Thomas Staubli, Feldeggstr 28, CH-3098 Konizn, Switzerland

INTRODUCTION

Athalya Brenner

The first *Feminist Companion to Samuel and Kings* was published in 1994. This second volume on the same Hebrew Bible (HB) books is published six years later. The second volume illustrates two facets— by no means the only ones—of the ongoing project of HB feminist criticism. The first is the continued preoccupation with female figures-in-the-text and their traditional male-related positions as daughters, wives, mothers, widows. The second point is the engaged dialogue with preceding feminist scholarship, exemplified for instance by the many references in this volume to essays in the first volume. In these senses, the present volume should be read as a second instalment and continuation of the first. Meanwhile, however, a growing body of literature has been devoted to gendered F/M sexuality in textuality. This is reflected in this volume as well, especially so in the first essay by Schroer and Staubli.

The nine essays collected here are arranged in the order of the main HB texts read in them. Nevertheless, as it happens, there also obtain interpretive links in each grouping. The four articles of Part I are about 1 and 2 Samuel texts and focus on sexuality and its socio-political consequences. The five essays in Part 2 are about 1 and 2 Kings texts and focus on encounters between women and holy men of god, with their consequences for reading gender relations in these so-called historiographical books.

Part I: Sexuality and Politics in the Books of Samuel

'Saul, David and Jonathan—The Story of a Triangle?', by Silvia Schroer and Thomas Staubli, is an exploration of HB attitudes to male homosexuality as applied to narratives about the three male figures grouped together in the Samuel texts. Recently homosexuality has been more openly discussed and redefined in biblical scholarship than previously, although the discussion is confined mostly to male homosexuality (as dictated by the lack of HB material about female homo-

sexuality.[1] Schroer and Staubli review the attempts made by commentators, mainly German ones, to waive as absurd suggestions of a
homosexual relationship between David and Jonathan.[2] They re-read
the relevant texts for love language and sexual language, concluding
that not only did David and Jonathan have a homoerotic and homosexual relationship, but probably also David and Saul. To further support their position, Schroer and Staubli cite examples of homoerotic
relations between apparently married men from ancient Egyptian
culture and artistic representation. Since most recent discussions of
male homosexuality in the HB lean towards the classical, Greco-
Roman, worlds for redefinitions, the present contribution is a welcome addition—and, of course, religiously and socially relevant to
contemporary concerns.

This volume has two essays by Lillian Klein, whose numerous
thoughtful contributions to the *Feminist Companion* First and Second
Series deserve special thanks from editor and readers alike. In the first
contribution, 'Michal, the Barren Wife', Klein notes that, unlike other
biblical once-barren women, 'Michal, however, remains infertile to the
end of her life. The singularity of Michal's marked identification as a
childless woman invites the reader to explore the sources and ramifications of her infertility.' Why does Michal remain barren in/by the
text? Michal, a complex figure of victim and strong woman at the
same time, appears to be unloved by both her father Saul and her
husband David, in whose battle for control and prestige she is little
better than a pawn. She loves David and acts on her commitment to
him. Why she does not go with the husband she helps escape from
her father is left unclear, as is her attitude to her second husband
Palti. Upon her return to David's household, a change has apparently
taken place. Michal appears bitter, resentful towards David, as the

1. Cf. pp. 139-44 in A. Brenner, *The Intercourse of Knowledge: On Gendering
Desire and 'Sexuality' in the Hebrew Bible* (Leiden: E.J. Brill, 1997) on male and female
sexuality and recent literature mentioned there.

2. Such scholarly waivers, delivered largely by male readers and commentators as a matter of course and conviction, reminds me of a recent furore in Israel.
Yael Dayan, a member of the Knesset (the Israeli parliament), referred in passing
to a homosexual tie between David and Jonathan during a Knesset debate on gay
civil rights. The result was a public outcry in defence of the 'maligned' biblical figures. Interestingly, not only orthodox and rabbinic circles voiced loud shock. The
so-called 'secular' Israeli public reacted similarly and with vehemence. Accused of
having tampered light-headedly with things sacred for Jews and Israelis, Yael
Dayan had to modify her rhetorically and politically naïve—albeit plausible—
statement.

story of the ark makes clear. Klein suggests that Michal's behaviour here, strongly condemned by the biblical narrative, implies a response to her circumstances, to the way she was used by both husband and father, so that from a loving wife she is transformed into a scornful shrew. But, Klein reminds us, Michal finally speaks up (which she has not done since she spoke to her father) to David: she regains her voice and, presumably as punishment for so doing, remains childless. An additional reason for her barrenness may be her association with the household gods (*t^erāpîm*) she uses to help David escape.

'Bathsheba Revealed', Klein's second essay, invites us to invert the way we view Bathsheba. Until the advent of feminist Bible criticism and beyond it, it has been customary for readers and scholars—especially male ones—to view Bathsheba as a scheming woman who seduces David by purposefully bathing on her roof, and to fantasize that she bathed in the nude (2 Sam. 11). Feminist scholars have repeatedly tried to cleanse Bathsheba from responsibility for seduction in her meeting with David, positing her as a victim of male lust and placing the responsibility for the chain of affairs leading to Solomon's death squarely on David. Having performed a close reading of the narrative, Klein directs us to its obvious intertexts—the narratives of Tamar and Ruth, the other significant women in the house of David's lineage. As a third step, Klein reads Bathsheba's involvement in Solomon's ascent to the throne (1 Kgs 1–2). Her provocative suggestion is that Bathsheba indeed shares responsibility and complicity with David, although his share is obviously greater than hers, since her prime motivation is to become a mother (to a son), much like Tamar and Ruth. Far from being a victim, Bathsheba does what is expected of any biblical woman—all she can do, honestly or otherwise, to become a mother. Her strength is apparent in the way she secures her son's reign too; and her motivation is implicitly justified by her becoming mother to a great king.

In 'Tamar and the "Coat of Many Colors" ', Adrien Bledstein studies the meaning of the *k^etonet passîm* that Tamar, daughter of David, wore when she came to the scene of her rape by Amnon and tore afterwards, in order to understand its significance for Tamar's story. She begins from the premise that the *k^etonet passîm* worn by both Joseph and Tamar, and only by them, must have similar symbolic-social and literal meanings.[3] An exploration of the linguistic desig-

3. On the symbolic implications of clothing in the HB, and esp. on clothing and gender, see Heather A. McKay, 'Gendering the Discourse of Display in the Hebrew Bible', in B. Becking and M. Dijkstra (eds.), *Gender-Specific and Related*

nation of both *kᵉtonet* and *passîm*, together with a study of the possible
social and religio-cultic significations of this clothing item, as gleaned
from material and literal evidence of ancient Mesopotamia, reveals
that the translation 'coat of many colours' is less than satisfactory.
Bringing together ancient Near Eastern evidence, Jewish sources and
a detailed reading of Tamar's story, Bledstein concludes on a personal
note:

> I cannot believe that this learned, gifted woman shriveled up and died
> in her brother Absalom's house. We are not told what happened to
> Tamar thereafter, as the Court History focuses on David and the demise
> of Absalom. I like to imagine that Tamar, like Joseph, came to under-
> stand her trauma and to use her gifts to benefit all Israel. The flounced
> garment distinguished her as a mistress of dreams. Her commission
> was to perform a ceremony to bring about healing. Bereft of the
> garment, she was free from the illusions woven into it by her father.

Finally, the essay ends with the citation of a Jewish prayer.

Part II: Women and Men of God in the Books of Kings

Four stories in which women play a significant role are read here. In
all, the women are mothers to a son whose life is in jeopardy: the son
is nameless in all but the first case (Abijah son of Jeroboam, 1 Kgs
14.1), and voiceless in all but the third case (2 Kgs 4.19[4]). In the first
(1 Kgs 14) and last (2 Kgs 6–7), the mother is positioned between a
king and a man of god. In the second (1 Kgs 17) and third (2 Kgs 4
and its sequel in 2 Kgs 8), 'she' eventually confronts a man of god
regarding her son. In the second and third cases, the fate of the
woman's son is reversed and he lives.

These textual mothers are depicted as agents of at least some independence, be they widows (the second and third cases) or married
women (Jeroboam hides behind his masked wife; the Shunamite's
husband is of little consequence to the plot of 2 Kgs 4 and 8) or of
unspecified marital status (the fourth case). They are nevertheless
nameless, as against the named man of god (if not necessarily the king

---

Studies in Memory of Fokkelien van Dijk-Hemmes (Leiden: E.J. Brill, 1996), pp. 169-99,
esp. pp. 170-71 and 179-83.

4.   The great woman's son here utters one word (in the Hebrew), twice
repeated: ‏ראשׁי ראשׁי‎, 'my head my head'. For a provocative analysis of this utter-
ance cf. F. van Dijk-Hemmes, 'The Great Woman of Shunem and the Man of God:
A Dual Interpretation of 2 Kings 4.8-37', in Athalya Brenner (ed.), *A Feminist
Companion to Samuel and Kings* (The Feminist Companion to the Bible, 5; Sheffield:
Sheffield Academic Press, 1994), pp. 218-30.

who, in 2 Kgs 6, is nameless as well). Adele Reinhartz explains, in her 'Anonymous Women and the Collapse of the Monarchy: A Study in Narrative Technique',[5] how not naming a woman while the narrated male figure is named is a point of technique that focuses attention on the male figure[s] and decentres the female figures. This is clearly applicable also to the textual 'sons'—their namelessness and voice-lessness are indications of their lower narrative status. But the women, with the exclusion of Jeroboam's wife who speaks only by implica-tion, are not voiceless. This added parameter is reason enough for re-examining these stories in which a mother is pitched against a man of god. The essays in this section, each in its own way, indeed re-evalu-ate Reinhartz's assertion for such narratives.

In 'Center or Fringe? Positioning the Wife of Jeroboam (1 Kings 14.1-18)', Uta Schmidt discusses the placing of Jeroboam's wife in between the two oppositional poles of narrative centrality and narra-tive marginality. Her approach is narratological, after Mieke Bal. By deploying a multi-layered narratological strategy, Schmidt is able to show how the ambivalence in the story causes the Wife to be at its centre and margin simultaneously. The woman is nameless and voice-less, yet the plot hinges on her actions. Her identity is vague and rela-tional (to her husband and child), and yet she has to dress up to hide it and is recognized nevertheless. She is placed with and among king, prophet and god—and yet, like many other biblical female figures, has no resting place at the narrative's end.

In 'The Widow of Zarephath and the great Woman of Shunem: A Comparative Analysis of Two Stories', Jopie Siebert-Hommes builds on and is in continuous dialogue with the late Fokkelien van Dijk-Hemmes's work on 'The Great Woman of Shunem and the Man of God: A Dual Interpretation of 2 Kings 4.8-37'. Siebert-Hommes focuses on the 'men of god', Elijah and Elisha, the chief and perhaps only protagonists of their respective stories. She performs a detailed struc-tural analysis of each story, then compares them to one another. Her conclusion is that Elisha's revival of the woman's son is emblematic of his status by comparison to his master Elijah: his stature as a man of god is relatively inferior; his revival of the great woman's son is but a shadow, perhaps a parody, of Elijah's revival of the widow's son. Whereas the widow need not push Elijah, and duly recognizes and reflects on his and his god's greatness, the great woman of Shunem has to push Elisha into reviving her son. In this way, she has a very important theological role to play: helping Elisha realize his destiny.

5. In Brenner (ed.), *A Feminist Companion to Samuel and Kings*, pp. 43-65.

This is her role in the narrative, to be a foil for Elisha's relatively inferior but nevertheless godly stature. As a remedial action of sorts, Siebert-Hommes suggests that the nameless woman be renamed גדולה, 'great'.

'Subverting a Man of God, Elevating a Woman: Role and Power Reversals in 2 Kings 4', by Mary Shields, was first published in 1993. In this essay, too, defining the woman's role vis-à-vis Elisha is taken up, and the analogy with 1 Kings 17 is not ignored. Shields agrees that on the surface of 2 Kings 4, the narrative is a miracle fabula enhancing the prestige of Elisha, the man of god. However, writes Shields, certain elements in the story itself and in its parallels, such as Elijah's revival of the widow's son, undermine the apparent surface meaning. A close reading will reveal a role reversal between the Shunamite woman and Elisha. Thus, Elisha is undermined as a man of god wheras the Shunamite woman's narrative status is ultimately elevated relative to his. Nevertheless, another reversal takes place in the story's ending and in the sequel or addition to it in 2 Kings 8. Finally and nonetheless, the ever-present and dominant patriarchal perspective subverts and minimizes the woman's power and status.

In her 'Self-response to "Subverting a Man of God, Elevating a Woman"', Mary Shields re-examines her position of several years ago. She is content with the close reading of the narrative that she attempted in that essay, but also recognizes how her reading was influenced by issues and even slogans feminist scholars espoused in the past and is thus firmly dated to concerns of that time. In the remainder of her self-response, Shileds engages in dialogue with a recent article by S. Brent Plate and E.M. Rodríguez Mangual. Building on her article and proceeding from Hélène Cixous' ideas about 'giving' and 'gifts', Plate and Rodríguez Mangual argue for the politics of power Elisha engages in in the narrative. Shields basically agrees with their analysis but wishes to refine the power dynamics of giving and receiving with regard to Elisha and the woman by rereading 2 Kgs 8.1-6 together with 2 Kings 4.

In 1 Kgs 3.16-28, two nameless 'prostitutes', mothers unattached to male relatives, come to King Solomon for judgment: both had baby sons; the one is dead, both claim ownership of the live one. Solomon, in his wisdom, decrees that the living baby be cut in two halves (lengthways? widthways? One is tempted to ask these pertinent questions), to be given to both claimants. The true biological mother gives up her claim so that the child lives. Although popular wisdom has it that the child is given to her, the syntax of v. 27—תנו לה, 'give *her*'— leaves the issue unclear. Also unclear is the 'wisdom' component of

Solomon's decree. Both problems—who gets the child? Is Solomon 'wise', as the text seem to claim for him?—remain with us in spite of the adulation expressed in v. 28.[6] In 'Cannibal Mothers and Me: A Mother's Reading of 2 Kings 6.24–7.20', Laurel Lanner reads, as a mother, a mothers-and-babies narrative that takes the 1 Kings 3 story further. This time, one of the babies has been eaten in time of siege and hunger; the second mother refuses to allow her own baby to be eaten; the nameless king is helpless, no resolution is possible, and the man of god (Elisha) has to be appealed to. It is all too easy to be deeply horrified by the cannibal mother, but Lanner tries to re-examine her position, her condemnation and victimization by author, editors and readers. What is the woman supposed to do when all the male figures in the story—god, Elisha, the king—are either remote and uncaring, or else impotent to help? How is she supposed to survive in the world those male figures have created? Lanner writes by way of conclusion:

> Elisha and God seem irredeemable from the woman's perspective. As with much theodicy there is room for anger toward God and God's representatives. Unfortunately for the woman, she cannot step out of the story and wonder if God has been co-opted into the Deuteronomist's theology, but I am not sure that would relieve her pain.

Her remarks, so it seems to me, are valid not only for the cannibal mother. They are valid for a very high percentage of the female figures and representations in the HB text.

At the very end of this truly horrifying narrative we read that Elisha, who together with the king and his God did not or would not prevent the maternal cannibalism, had saved another woman and her son—possibly the Shunamite woman whose son is revived in 2 Kings 4 (and see Shields's and Siebert-Hommes's essays in this volume)—from the same famine. The woman returns after the war, goes to the king and receives her lands and property back by royal decree and because of Elisha's fame (2 Kgs 8.1-6). We have no way of knowing

---

6.   As already in rabbinic sources—see *Gen. R.* 95.12, *Cant. R.* 1, *Qoh. R.* 10.1, *Midr. Teh.* to Ps 72, and *b. Mak.* 23.2. It seems that three loci of hesitation are present for the sages: whether the women were indeed 'prostitutes'; whether the procedure followed by Solomon was a correct legal procedure (no witnesses); and how he knew who the true mother (biological or otherwise) was. A *bat qôl*, a (feminine!) voice from heaven, has to be enlisted for instructing Solomon as to the mother's identity, thus detracting from his own credibility as 'wise'. Nevertheless, ultimately his wisdom is not questioned, although it is implied that his conduct and moral fibre are.

Part I

SEXUALITY AND POLITICS IN THE BOOKS OF SAMUEL

SAUL, DAVID AND JONATHAN—THE STORY OF A TRIANGLE? A CONTRIBUTION TO THE ISSUE OF HOMOSEXUALITY IN THE FIRST TESTAMENT[*]

Silvia Schroer and Thomas Staubli

Recent Interpretation—Still Afflicted with Taboos

David and Jonathan shared a homoerotic and, more than likely, a homosexual relationship. The books of Samuel recount the love of the two men with utter frankness. In his song mourning the death of the beloved, David explicitly ranks the love of men he experienced with Jonathan above the love of women (2 Sam. 1.26).

The need to make more than a few statements in passing about the love between two men, in the early period of the Israelite Monarchy, has to do with the fact that homosexuality is still very much a taboo. Our society clings to the ideology of a 'natural' heterosexuality; only recently has some movement on this subject entered into the (Protestant) churches. None of the German-language commentaries on the books of Samuel that have appeared in recent years has succeeded in removing this shadow. Resorting to more or less explicit mystification of language, they all defend themselves against the assumption which the text itself nearly compels us to make, namely, that it speaks of a homosexual relationship.[1] Commenting on 2 Sam. 1.26, Fritz Stolz writes:

[*]   Translated by Barbara and Martin Rumscheidt.
1.   A laudable exception is the sermon delivered by Willy Schottroff at the German Kirchentag in 1987. It contains numerous individual observations and basic ideas on the topic of 'love between people of the same sex'. (Cf. 'Gleichgeschlechtliche Liebe', in Luise and Willy Schottroff, *Die Macht der Auferstehung: Sozialgeschichtliche Bibelauslegungen* [Munich: Chr. Kaiser Verlag, 1988], pp. 126-32). In the English-speaking world this discussion has been much more open and involved for a longer time. The still very readable monograph by Tom Horner, *Jonathan Loved David: Homosexuality in Biblical Times* appeared as early as 1978 in Philadelphia (Westminster Press). However, his chapter on David and Jonathan lacks a thorough examination of the texts. Interestingly, poets such as Else Lasker Schüler and Bertolt Brecht have recognized David and Jonathan as lovers.

Of course, the text is not to be understood in the sense of homosexuality. It was common in Greece, but shunned in Israel and prohibited under pain of death (cf. Lev. 18.22). What the text portrays is, rather, the affection of friends who, together, have experienced the first phase of manhood and whose relationship survived every change that fate imposed on them.[2]

Georg Hentschel says this about the same verse: 'In the moment of mourning, David even admits that the bond with Jonathan meant more to him than anything else. But since right into his old age David was drawn to women, his relationship to Jonathan can hardly be misunderstood as a homosexual one (cf. Lev. 18.22; 20.13)'.[3] The apologetic argumentation found here is governed by two (widespread) erroneous conclusions.

1. The prescriptive regulations in Leviticus concerning homosexuality are held to be descriptive portrayals of a much earlier social reality. However, in most instances, a regulation is to be understood as an indication that reality did not match what the biblical authors wanted it to be. (A similar mechanism of confusion is at work, for example, in relation to the prohibition of images, on the one hand, and the existence of pictorial art, on the other.)

2. When a man can be shown to have had relations with several women and, in this case, entered into marriage, it is assumed that he could not have had homophile tendencies. But there certainly are human beings who feel attracted to both sexes. More importantly, it must be remembered that in ancient Israel marriages were often, if not necessarily always, not love marriages. In this connection (and in others), much could be said concerning David's relations with women. It is quite conceivable that an Israelite in such an important position had several wives—a whole harem, for that matter—without these marriages having much to do with love. Rather, they had to do with politics, progeny and, of course, social norms.

As far as the love between David and Jonathan is concerned, it is conceivable that stories about it were not received simply and blindly. The political dimensions of that relationship for the person and position of Saul were always made apparent. After all, it was at the small court of Saul where all this took place. But even so, Saul is

2.   *Das erste und zweite Buch Samuel* (ZBK–AT, 9; Zürich: Theologischer Verlag, 1981), p. 189.

3.   *2 Samuel* (Die Neue Echter Bibel, Kommentar zum Alten Testament; Würzburg: Echter Verlag, 1884), p. 8. H.-J. Stoebe's *Das zweite Buch Samuels* (KAT, 8.2: Gütersloh: Gütersloher Verlagshaus/Gerd Mohn, 1994) does not budge one inch from the traditional patterns of reading; cf. esp. pp. 96 onwards.

utterly neglected when it comes to the love of these two men. However, since nowhere in the narrative is Saul's relationship to David recited without emotion, it is worth considering whether the relationship of these men with each other does not have a lot to do with love, passion and jealousy. Among many other things, the answer to that question depends on how one understands and assesses what else the First Testament says about homosexuality.

Homosexuality in the First Testament[4]

Unlike men's homosexuality, the First Testament does not address women's homosexuality in terms of laws. The book of Ruth narrates as a matter of course the faithful life companionship of two women who loved each other (4.15). But when it comes to male homosexuality, the narratives speak of it in terms of laws. In Genesis 19 (of Lot and his family in Sodom) and Judges 19 (the violence at Gibeah) we are told about the male population of certain towns demanding that a host hand over a foreign male visitor, so that they may assault him sexually. In both instances the sexual assault on the men is averted by having the sexual craving of the violators assuaged through an abuse of a woman.[5] With reference to two legal clauses in the holiness code (Lev. 18.22 and 20.13), many commentators have asserted and still assert to this day that homosexuality was taboo for the First Testament. But what do these laws from the sixth century BCE actually prohibit?

> You are not to lie with someone male as with a woman: it would be an abomination (18.22).

---

4.   This theme can be addressed now in summary fashion only. The reader is referred to the very detailed study in Erhard S. Gerstenberger's excellent expert opinion, prepared for the Protestant churches: 'Homosexualität im Alten Testament: Geschichte und Bewertungen', in Evangelische Kirche in Hessen und Nassau (ed.), *Lesben, Schwule, … Kirche. Homosexualität und kirchliches Handeln: Texte aus Kirche und Wissenschaft* (Frankfurt, 1996).

5.   Gen. 9.20-27 (Canaan staring at his naked father, drunk and asleep in his tent) is an etiology of the Israelites' hatred for the Canaanites and, most likely, a reference to a Canaanite culture of homosexuality. In one and the same breath, Deut. 23.18-19 forbids female and male dedicatees to the service of the house of God. Most translations are based on the assumption that these women and men were cultic prostitutes; however, the Hebrew text does not make that clear. Even the notion that is to be found in certain prophetic writings, namely 'harloting away from YHWH', cannot be directly connected to these men and women serving in the cult, since that notion is used metaphorically already by Hosea (e.g. 4.12-19).

> When a man lies with someone male as one lies with a woman, both
> have committed an abomination and both shall suffer the penalty of
> death; their blood shall come upon them (20.13).

The law prohibits that a man satisfy his sexual appetite by means of
anal intercourse with another man. The issue within the context of the
holiness code is the ordering of the world in terms of 'pure' and 'impure'.[6] The law's context is a whole series of sexual taboos. What is
repudiated here is that a man do with another man what a man 'normally' does with a woman. The 'normality' of this order is further sup-
ported by the argument that the indigenous people of Canaan are said
to have defiled themselves on account of these sexual practices. (Lev.
18.3, 24; 20.23). Thus, the law condemns homosexual deviations within
what it sanctifies as heterosexual normalcy. The issue is not a moral-
ethical renunciation of a homosexual culture or a judgment upon a
relationship between men, since that is not something that lies in the
purview of what the law-makers had in mind. Nor is it primarily a
matter of penal sanctions against homosexuals (Lev. 18.22 prescribes
no sanctions whatsoever). The law is interested wholly in purity and
impurity. In addition, it is quite likely that what the law has especially
in view is the violent aspects of sex between men which we know
from the above-mentioned narratives of sexual assault (Gen. 19; Judg.
19). A comparison with a law from middle Assyria, from the rule of
Tiglath-pileser I (1115–1076 BCE), would confirm this:

> When a man lies with his comrade and it has been confirmed and he is
> found guilty, he is to be lain with and castrated.

This is obviously not about the homosexuality of two consenting partners, but about a sexual act of humiliation, of satisfying an appetite
and thirst for power.[7] The offence described corresponds most closely
to what our legislations call 'coercive sex'; as in, for example,
Switzerland's Criminal Code, article 189:

---

6.   According to Lev. 18.22, the crime is terminologically not one of the things
that make for cultic impurity, contrary to bestiality (intercourse with an animal)
which is mentioned immediately afterwards. Intercourse of a male with another
male is a forbidden 'abomination' but does not make one impure. (Cf. the analogic
categorization of animals in Lev. 11. Jacob Milgrom provides more detail in his
Leviticus 1–16 [AB, 3; Garden City, NY: Doubleday, 1991], pp. 656 onwards.)

7.   On this function of practised homosexuality, in use to this day in the Middle East, cf. the chapter on homosexuality in the study of the Iraqi scholar A. Al-
Wardi, *Soziologie des Nomadentums* (Neuwied: Luchterhand, 1972).

> Whoever coerces another person with threats, force and psychological
> pressure into intercourse-like or other sexual acts, will be punished with
> prison or correctional institution...

In short, what the two articles of law in Leviticus have in mind is
not partnership-like mutual relationships, as homosexual persons in
our contemporary cultural context desire and seek to achieve. Rather,
they are concerned with a heterosexual 'norm' within which (violent)
homosexual acts on the part of men are experienced as 'gruesome' in
the highest degree. Herbert Haag and Katharina Elliger draw the following conclusions:

> The Bible did not know homosexuality as a disposition that shapes
> human beings. Rather, in every instance it speaks of purely sexual con-
> tacts and not of permanent love-relationships, or of values of the soul
> and spirit that for us today may be part of homosexuality. And that is
> why today, we cannot avail ourselves of the First Testament's repudi-
> ation as a theologically conclusive argument against homosexuality.[8]

Today, Haag and Elliger's conclusion is taken up with gratitude by
homosexual persons.[9] It is experienced as liberating because it minimizes the significance of First Testament texts for the condemnation
of homosexuality as it is understood by the gays among us. It facil-
itates the approach to the recognition of genuine homosexual love,
which is a cause for joy. But, on the other hand, it impedes the search
for positive homosexual role models within the Bible. For many religious homosexual persons who search the Scriptures for their roots, it
is natural to see in David and Jonathan their role models, since to this
day their story awakens our sympathy. But the exegetes' conclusions
create obstacles to gays seeing these two men as a genuinely
homosexual couple. In his recent study, Jens Weizer still claims that
'the friendship of David and Jonathan attested to in the Bible was no
gay relationship (in the historical sense). And yet, in a certain sense it
was perhaps on the way to being just that.'[10] Does such a statement
do justice to the biblical texts? The answer is to be provided by a
detailed and careful reading of the David–Jonathan–Saul narratives.

---

8.   Herbert Haag and Katharina Elliger, *'Stört nicht die Liebe': Die Diskriminierung der Sexualität—ein Verrat an der Bibel* (Olten: Walter Verlag, 1986), p. 145.

9.   Jens Weizer, *Vom anderen Ufer: Schwule fordern Heimat in der Kirche* (Düssel-
dorff: Patmos Verlag, 1995), p. 106 onwards.

10.   Weizer, *Vom anderen Ufer*, p. 190.

A Study of the Texts

Approaching the texts with pre-judgment, translators of and commentators on the books of Samuel have eliminated many an erotic note and association even in their translations. The Hebrew word for 'to love' (אהב) plays, among other factors, a significant role here; it is context-dependent, much like the corresponding English word. It embraces a similarly broad spectrum and can have more, or less, erotic nuances.[11]

According to 1 Sam. 16.14-23, David comes as a music therapist to the court of Saul, who is already suffering from depression.[12] Another tradition is woven into this one, namely that David arrived with the reputation of being an accomplished warrior (cf. 1 Sam. 17):

> So it was that David came to Saul and entered his service. Saul came to love him very much (ויאהבהו) and made him his armour-bearer. Saul sent to Jesse saying, 'let David remain in my service, for he has found favour in my sight' (כי מצא חן בעיני) (16.21-22).

In the ancient Near East, to be someone's armour-bearer or adjutant always signified a position of absolute trust for, to a large extent, life and death could indeed depend on the closest battle companion of a high-ranking warrior. That Saul came to love David may well correspond to the sentiment contained in the story of David's rise to power, that 'everybody loved David'. But here, this 'love' is made into an important aspect of why Saul had such great confidence in David. The phrase 'to find favour in one's sight' may, indeed, be understood in the sense of condescending political favour, as a show of good will on the part of someone in a superior rank; yet the Hebrew idiom never entirely lost the nuance of fondness (cf. 1 Sam. 20.3). The very same formulation is to be found in Deut. 24.1, where the issue is that a woman no longer finds favour in the sight of her partner in marriage (and cf. Est. 5.2). 1 Samuel 18.2 ('And Saul took him [David] that day

---

11.   J.A. Thompson's study, 'The Significance of the Verb Love in the David-Jonathan Narratives in 1 Samuel', *VT* 24 (1974), pp. 334-38, shows that an examination of the word אהב and its verbal cognates offers no help in coming to a decision concerning the nature of David and Jonathan's relationship.

12.   Both in its flow, and in numerous details, this narrative resembles the narrative of the aging David, for whom his officials are seeking a woman to 'warm him', another form of therapy. But while the beautiful Abishag unduly aroused the interpreters' erotic fantasies and also prevented them from seeing what position of power she held, the opposite was the case when they came to interpret 1 Sam. 16.14-23.

to himself and did not let him return to his father's house') flirts with
innuendo, to say the least, for it was customary in Israel for a man to
take a woman to himself and only in extraordinary circumstances,
such as widowhood or irreconcilability, would she return to her father's house (Gen. 38.11; Lev. 22.13; Judg. 19.2).

The intimate relationship between David and Jonathan is initially
addressed in 1 Samuel 18, the very same chapter that also speaks for
the first time of Saul's disfavour toward David and a first attempt to
murder him. In 18.1-16, Saul's jealousy is explicitly explained: David
achieved greater success in the wars against the Philistines and, for
that reason, was more popular than Saul among the men and women
of Israel. But it is quite possible that the love relationship between
David and Saul's son, which in the narrative context comes like a bolt
out of the blue, has something to do with Saul's hatred. After all, it is
from this passion that it arises. From the outset, Jonathan is fascinated
with David:

> When his conversation with Saul had concluded, the *nepeš* (נֶפֶשׁ) of
> Jonathan was bound to the *nepeš* of David, and Jonathan came to love
> him (וַיֶּאֱהָבֵהוּ) as his own *nepeš*... Jonathan made a covenant with David
> because he loved him as his own *nepeš* (18.1-3).

Now, in this text and in most others, the Hebrew word *nepeš* is not
well translated as 'soul'; in its original sense, *nepeš* means the yearning
throat and, in a derivative sense, the craving, drive-like and life-seek-
ing aspects of human existence—such as the survival instinct (Prov.
16.26) or the sex drive (Gen. 34.2-3) and yearning desire. Jonathan
desires David and loves him as his own life. That it is a relationship of
erotic love we encounter here is suggested by the very similar words
the woman in the Song of Songs chooses for her beloved (1.17 and
four times in 3.1-4). She calls him 'the one whom my *nepeš* loves',
that is, the one whom she loves with all her passion and is desperately
searching for. The erotic character of Jonathan's affection is also
underlined in 1 Sam. 19.1, once again in direct connection with Saul's
murderous brooding:

> Now, Saul spoke to Jonathan, his son, and to all his servants about
> killing David. But Jonathan, David's son, delighted much in David
> (חָפֵץ בְּדָוִד).

The expression 'to delight in' (...בְּ חָפֵץ) has sexual connotations both
in Gen. 34.19, which tells of Shechem's delight in Dinah, and Deut.
21.14, which is about the appropriate ordering of the relations between free Israelite men and women prisoners of war. Deuteronomy
21 addresses the situation of such a woman in whom, after a certain

length of time, the man no longer takes delight, and what has to be done for her protection.

After Michal, David's first wife, had saved her partner from the raging Saul (1 Sam. 19.8-17), Jonathan proves his love for David by protecting him against another of Saul's attempts on his life (1 Sam. 20). In this part of the narrative we repeatedly find affirmations of Jonathan's love as well as of the pledges and the covenant he and David had made. David assumes that Saul knows about their relationship (20.1-4). A complicated plan is hatched for uncovering Saul's true intentions. The lovers' discussions and meetings take place out in the field:

> Jonathan said to David, 'Come, let us go out into the field' (ולכה ונצא השדה). So they both went out into the field (20.11).

Now, the field—uncultivated, unsettled land—is a place of hiding and refuge as well as the location of all sorts of meetings and events. All who want to be alone, to get away from civilization, go out into the field (cf. Cain and Abel in Gen. 4.18). Among those are lovers (cf. Ruth and Boaz, Ruth 3). It is with exactly the same words that the woman in Song 7.11 bids her beloved:

> Come, my beloved, let us go out into the field (לכה דודי נצא השדה).

It is in the field that the two men bid each other farewell; they kiss each other and weep together after David had bowed down in gratitude before his friend:

> They kissed one another and wept much for one another (1 Sam. 20.41b).

The references in 20.17 and 20.42 to swearing an oath recalls Song 2.7 and 8.4. The narrative indicates that the relationship between the two men is public knowledge even though it is not lived out openly. A similar situation is depicted in Song 8.1; here the woman wishes that her beloved were her brother so that she could kiss him in public.

Saul's angry reaction to David's absence from the feast of the new moon and to Jonathan's excuses is informative in this connection:

> Then Saul's anger flared up against Jonathan and he said to him: 'You son of a woman of no virtue whatever (בן נעות המרדות), I know full well that you have a liaison with the son of Jesse to your own shame (לבשתך) and to the shame of your mother's nakedness (לבשת ערות אמך)' (20.30).

Saul qualifies the relationship with wild indignities against his son. 'Son of a woman of no virtue' could mean something like 'son of a bitch', without indicating whether this is meant as an actual attack on

Jonathan's mother. בשת, 'shame, dishonouring' is the consequence of
this liaison in Saul's eyes. The issue here is not only the political
scandal of a royal son betraying father and kingdom for the sake of a
stranger, but also the effrontery of this homosexual love. By his action,
Jonathan shames his own mother; he 'uncovers her nakedness'. We
find very similar phrases repeatedly in Leviticus 20, where various
forms of forbidden sexual relationships within the extended family
and other sexual taboos are addressed. Behind these prohibitions is
the notion that on account of an offence, such as intercourse with an
aunt (Lev. 20.20), a man illegitimately disrupts the domain of intimacy of another man, in this case his uncle; to be precise, in this manner the offended man's 'nakedness (ערוה) is uncovered'. As far as Saul
is concerned, Jonathan's perversion profoundly affects not only Saul's
own honour but also the honour of Jonathan's mother.[13]

According to the narrative, David and Jonathan's farewell out in
the field was final, their ways parting for good. David mourns the
death of Saul and Jonathan on the battlefield of Gilboa in a song of
lamentation (2 Sam. 1.19-27); its second to last verse is dedicated to
Jonathan alone:

> I am in pain because of you, my brother Jonathan. You were a great
> delight to me (נעמת), more wonderful to me was your love than the love
> of women (1.26).

In v. 23, David had called Saul and Jonathan 'beloved'. In this fare-
well-verse, too, the poetry of love is not absent.[14] In Egyptian love
lyrics, but also in Israel, lovers referred to one another as 'brother' and
'sister' out of a sense of relatedness and belonging.[15] The root *n'm*
(נעם), 'to be delightful, lovely' is used in the Song of Songs in reference to the beloved man (1.16) and to the beloved woman (7.7). There,
the man and the woman experience each other as beautiful and as the
source of pure wellbeing. David calls the love he received from Jonathan 'wonderful' (נפלאתה), just as in Prov. 30.18 the love of a man for

---

13. It matches the ambivalence with which 1 Samuel portrays Saul: it has him
speak of shame at this very point, after having himself taken delight in David. One
only needs to compare how Saul, putting questions to the woman necromancer at
Endor (1 Sam. 28), contravenes his own edicts.

14. It is not astonishing that a declaration of love goes hand in hand with a
lamentation of death—seeing that, according to Song 8.6, love is the only effective
adversary of death.

15. Othmar Keel, *Das Hohelied* (ZBK-AT, 18; Zürich: Theologischer Verlag,
1986), pp. 152-53.

a woman is counted among the wondrous things that are really too lofty or wonderful (נִפְלָאוּ) to be comprehended.

David, Jonathan and Saul within the Purview of Egyptian and Aegean Homosexual Culture and Mesopotamian Literature

Anyone reading these Samuel texts through the lens of a biblical law code of the sixth century BCE on the subject of 'coercive sex', a code marked by Syrian influence, will fail to understand them. For the horizon of these texts about David and Saul and Jonathan is the culture of Egypt and the Aegean of the early first millennium BCE.

Egyptian culture under the Ramessids dominated Palestine of the thirteenth–twelfth centuries BCE. Homosexuality is not named in the Egyptian catalogues of sins. One may conclude, therefore, that homosexual relationships were tolerated, even though they were rare. Frequently, a male prostitute is unambiguously repudiated, as is homosexual rape, although in the myth of Set and Horus it is Horus who, having been sexually assaulted by Set, has to bear the shame. Among human beings it is, rather, the perpetrator who more often has to bear the shame.[16] Whereas textual sources often remain enigmatic, a number of Egyptian pictorial documents provide somewhat more information about men's homosexuality in Egypt. But even in this area of research the topic is taboo-laden so that, in the first instance, there exist no major studies; and, secondly, where there are quite evident indications, there reigns bashful silence.

The clearest example of such a process of dispossession is the publication by Ahmed M. Moussa and Hartwig Altenmüller on the common tomb or *mastaba* of Ne-ankhkhnum and Khnumhotep in Saqqarah, built in 2350 BCE.[17] The two buried men were in charge of the king's manicurists and certainly were part of the well-situated civil service. Their parents and siblings were employed in the weaving industry. Both men were married and had children. In their common *mastaba*, both had arranged for the following inscription to be placed:

> ...his wife, whom he loves, the administrator of the king's treasure,
> ...priestess of Hathor, Ruler of the Sycamore.

Except for the traditional wall-carving of a hunt in the swamp-lands and of a sacrificial offering on the death of someone, the two men never allowed themselves to be painted with their marriage partners

16. LA II, 1272-73.
17. *Das Grab des Nianchchnum und Chnumhotep* (Mainz: Philipp von Zabern Verlag, 1977).

Khentikaus and Khenutresp. Rather, every scene depicted appears twice, with each showing one of the two men buried in the *mastaba*. Three times in the wall carvings the two are shown in intimate embrace; several times we see them holding hands. An intimate embrace in which the noses touch (which, in light of the very reticent Egyptian convention, must be interpreted as a kiss) is to be found in *mastabas* of private individuals from the Old Kingdom only in connection with married couples or mothers or daughters. Apart from wall carvings or drawings in tombs, this mode of embrace often depicts the bond between the king and a deity.

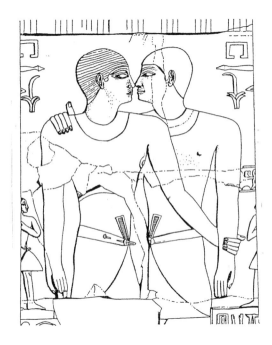

Figure 1. Ne-ankhkhnum and Khnumhotep as a couple. One of the three wall carvings in their tomb depicts the two men embracing, on the west side of the chamber (Fifth Dynasty, c. 2350 BCE). Drawing by Ines Haselbach, from Moussa and Altenmüller, *Das Grab des Nianchchnum und Chnumhotep.*

The tomb of Ne-ankhkhnum and Khnumhotep is a unique document. It shows that homoerotic relationships between men were practised and that, as in this case, the men also honoured social convention. Both men lived in regular marriage relationships and had children. The detailed inscriptions in the tomb contain no references whatever to the relationship with the friend, only the pictures tell of a love between two men that was to last beyond death. Subsequent generations obviously understood this message. With gypsum, they blotted out the picture of Khentikaus in one of the wall carvings depicting a sacrifice for the dead, where she is seated with Ne-ankh-khnum at a dining table. In their work on this tomb Moussa and Altenmüller nowhere speak of homosexuality; they do not even use the word in a footnote. They do discuss whether the two men might have been brothers or twins, although neither the tomb itself nor other parallel cases offer any real proof of that. And even if the men had been relatives, it would not rule out that they were a couple, given that in Egypt there were marriages between siblings.

From the period of the New Kingdom there is at least one additional pictorial document that depicts certain openness toward intimacy among men. In the tomb of the high-ranking civil servant Ramose in Thebes (c. 1365 BCE), a wall carving of a banquet shows a number of married couples, all of whose names are given. At the left end of them two young noblemen are seated, holding hands. One is named 'Keshy, Principal of the hunters of Amon'; the other is anonymous (see Figure 2). This finding also provides evidence that in Egypt male couples were openly accepted up to a certain degree, although they could never attain the same status as married couples.

In the twelfth century peoples from the Aegean colonized the coastal regions of Palestine. They showed themselves to be the dominant forces of the land until, under David's leadership, the tribes from the hill country gradually developed into a culture with remarkable political influence. David owes much to the Philistines. He learned from the enemy what was to help him, eventually, to triumph over them (1 Sam. 27, 29). Saul's court too viewed the Philistines as a model to be copied. There were no other models within reach. For example, weapons had to be bought from the Philistines (1 Sam. 13.19-22). And the people of Judah would not have limited their attention only to things military and technological. It is hardly necessary by now to show in detail that Mediterranean peoples of that time took homosexuality for granted.[18] Paedophilia (between teacher and student) blossomed— particularly in the military and in the academy, where men were

18. The anthology edited by Andreas K. Siems, *Sexualität und Erotik in der Antike* (WdF, 605; Darmstadt: Wissenschaftliche Buchgesellschaft, 1988), has a number of studies on this subject in classical antiquity. On homoeroticism in Greek art, cf. Angela Dierichs, *Erotik in der Kunst Griechenlands* (Mainz: Philipp von Zabern, 1993).

among themselves. So too did erotic friendship between young men and comrades-in-arms. But this is precisely the ambience of the narratives about Saul's court. An example of love between two men which the biblical narrative calls to mind is that of the friendship between Achilles and Patroclus. There too the primary themes, lovingly developed, are brotherhood in arms (*Iliad* 11.830 onwards), comradeship of unconditional faithfulness (1.345) and mourning for the deceased friend (18.98 onwards). That this friendship was understood in Greece as an erotic friendship is shown in the manner Aeschylus treated it. He referred to Patroclus as the one whom Achilles loves (*eromenos*); Plato describes Patroclus as the older lover (*erastes*) and teacher of the younger Achilles. The biblical narrative elegantly succeeds in showing David at one time in the role of (Saul's) lover and, at another, in that of the friend who experiences the favour of (Jonathan's) faithful friendship.

Figure 2. Keshy, principal of the hunters of Amon, with his friend at a festive meal. Relief on the wall of the entrance to the hall of pillars in the tomb of Ramose in Thebes (Thirteenth Dynasty, c. 1365 BCE). Kurt Lange and Max Hirmer, *Ägypten—Architektur, Plastik, Malerei in drei Jahrtausenden* (Munich: Hirmer Verlag, 1967), plate 17.3. Drawing by Ines Haselbach from Claude Vandersleyen, *Das Alte Ägypten* (Berlin: Propyläen Verlag, 1975), plate 293.

However, the writers of the David narrative were probably more familiar with the *Gilgamesh Epic*, a fragment of which was found in the rubble of Meggido, than with the epics of Greece which came into their 'Homeric' form only in the course of the eighth century BCE. It is not uncommon to encounter explicitly homosexual motifs in the description of the friendship between Gilgamesh and Enkidu. Gilgamesh repeatedly dreams of making love with Enkidu.[19] The men kiss, embrace and touch each other.[20] Gilgamesh falls asleep on his friend's thighs[21] and dreams, later comparing him to a paramour;[22] finally, Gilgamesh mourns for Enkidu in language that comes very close to David's lamenting the loss of Jonathan:

> [My friend, whom I loved so dearly] who went with me through every hardship, Enkidu, whom I loved so dearly and who went with me through every hardship, has succumbed to the fate of humankind...[23]

Conclusion

In the Egyptian culture which prevailed in the Palestine of the second half of the second millennium BCE, homosexuality between men was indeed a marginal phenomenon. However, it was not condemned and, at times, even became the subject of artistic representation. The culture of the Philistines, which prevailed at the turn of the millennium, cultivated relationships among men within the context of Mediterranean homoeroticism. Therefore, it is no coincidence that this theme emerges in the Bible exactly within the narratives of David, from which we also receive most of the information concerning the

19. Cf. *ANET*, p. 76.

20. Cf. *ANET*: 'They kissed each other and formed a friendship' (p. 79); 'Grasping each other, hand in hand...' (p. 81); 'They grasped each other for their nightly rest' (p. 82); 'They embraced each other as they went on...' (p. 85); 'They embraced and kissed each other' (p. 98). Note further the text in which Enkidu mourns the decaying of his physical body in recollection of their joyful intimacy: '[My body...], which thou didst touch as thy heart rejoiced, Vermin devour [as though] an old garment. [My body...], which thou didst touch as thy heart rejoiced, [...] is filled with dust' (p. 99); and the reference to Enkidu as the 'bosom friend' of Gilgamesh (p. 86).

21. Cf. *ANET*, p. 83. The slightly different interpretation of the authors is based on the text as rendered in TUAT III, p. 691, which translates 'thighs' instead of 'knees'.

22. *ANET*, p. 82 regards the passus in question as unintelligible. The interpretation of the authors is based on TUAT III, p. 693.

23. Translated by the authors following TUAT III, p. 665. Cf. the repetitive occurrence of the motive in *ANET*, p. 89-92.

Philistines. When the sages of Jerusalem were composing the story of
the David–Saul–Jonathan triangle in its written form, and were
searching for literary models, they could draw upon their own, indigenous poetry of heterosexual love and, when needed, on the *Gilgamesh Epic* from Mesopotamia.

On the basis of such a changed perspective on the subject of
homosexuality in the biblical tradition, one would, of course, go on to
explore why it was at all important for the authors of the books of
Samuel to bring up these relationships among men within the context
of a political history. Why should these things be preserved for
posterity? Is there not a kind of morality mirror behind so many of
these books' narratives? One thing is certain: when these stories were
written down, it was no scandal that a King David had matured
through such relationships. In this matter, the books of Samuel are
quite a bit ahead of our allegedly enlightened times.[24]

24. The past few years have seen a lively discussion on 'Homosexuality and
the Bible'. At the present moment we would opt for a higher differentiated
terminology (homoeroticism/homosexuality), following Nissininen.

On the basis of the discussion between Stone and Carden, we would go even
further in denying any relevance of Gen. 19 and Judg. 19 for the topic. Zehnder's
contribution is another example of ideological abuse of word statistics; this author
seems not to appreciate our attempt to adduce new historical insights to the
discussion.

Being unable to discuss the most recent contributions in the present context in
more detail, we would nevertheless wish to list them: M. Zehnder, 'Exegetische
Beobachtungen zu den David-Jonathan-Geschichten', *Bib* 79 (1998), pp. 153-79;
M. Nissinen, 'Die Liebe von David und Jonatan als Frage der modernen Exegese',
Bib 80 (1999), pp. 250-63; D.J. Wold, *Out of Order: Homosexuality in the Bible and the
Ancient Near East* (Grand Rapids: Baker Book House, 1998); M. Nissinen *Homoeroti-
cism in the Biblical World: A Historical Perspective* (Minneapolis: Fortress Press, 1998);
K. Stone, 'Gender and Homosexuality in Judges 19: Subject-Honor, Object-Shame?',
JSOT 67 (1995), pp. 87-107; M. Carden, 'Homophobia and Rape in Sodom and
Gebeah: A Response to Ken Stone', *JSOT* 82 (1999), pp. 83-96; H.C. Washington,
'Violence and the Construction of Gender in the Hebrew Bible: A New Historicist
Approach', *BibInt* 5 (1997), pp. 324-63; K. Hoheisel, Art. 'Homosexualität', *Reallexi-
kon für Antike und Christentum* 16 (1994), pp. 289-364; E. Hartmann, 'Homosexual-
ität', *Der Neue Pauly* 5 (1998), pp. 703-707.

MICHAL, THE BARREN WIFE

Lillian R. Klein

David's procreativity is substantiated by the sons he fathers by each of his many wives[1]—with the singular exception of his wife Michal, who remains childless 'to her dying day' (2 Sam. 6.23). It seems clear that the infertility in this instance lies with the woman, with Michal,[2] but there still remains the significance of her infertility. In biblical texts women may be 'forgotten' by God, as Sarah is (Gen. 17.17),[3] or they may fail to conceive because God favors another woman's conception, as Rachel is barren while her sister Leah repeatedly bears sons (Gen. 29.31). God usually remembers or rectifies his judgment, resulting in the woman's long-delayed and much-anticipated pregnancy (e.g. Gen. 30.22). Michal, however, remains infertile to the end of her life. The singularity of Michal's marked identification as a childless woman invites the reader to explore the sources and ramifications of her infertility.[4]

David is still a young man, as yet unmarried, and, as he puts it, 'a poor man of no consequence' (1 Sam. 18.23) when Saul offers his daughter Michal to him as wife. In fact, Michal is the second daughter Saul offers to David as wife. The daughter first offered, Merab, was the older, and—for no obvious reason—was instead given to another man.

Michal, we recall, is 'given' to David by Saul, much as an object is given, and with the intention not of gaining a son-in-law but of disposing of David as a threat. In fact, Saul plots that Michal will serve as

---

1.   Daughters, such as Tamar, are mentioned only as they appear in narrative texts.

2.   Biblical texts do not admit to the possibility of male infertility among Israelites.

3.   Sarah is 90 years old when she first conceives (Gen. 17.17).

4.   Sarah (Gen. 11.30) is forgotten, and Rachel is neglected in favor of Leah (Gen. 29.31). Both women are later 'remembered'. Hannah (1 Sam. 2.21) gains pregnancy by prayer.

a 'snare' to put David in a vulnerable position against the Philistines
(1 Sam. 18.21). In effect, Saul gives Michal in marriage to David with
the plan that David will be killed, thereby preventing the marriage.
And when David and Michal *do* marry, Saul's intention is to widow
his daughter, to kill his daughter's husband, whom she loves. Michal
is thus caught in a triangle with her father and her husband, with Saul
persecuting David out of jealousy. Saul's relationship to Michal is
clearly less important to him than his jealousy of David. These mes-
sages from father to daughter do not show love or esteem, and they
surely impinge upon Michal's perception of herself.

Furthermore, Michal is not described as 'beautiful' like two of
David's other significant wives, Abigail and Bathsheba. Indeed, David
is nowhere described as even being attracted to Michal. The text suggests he marries her for his advantage: 'David was pleased with
becoming the king's son-in-law' (1 Sam. 18.26). On the other hand,
Michal is twice reported as loving David (1 Sam. 18.20, 28).[5] Michal's
position is not difficult to infer. She has not received love and validation from her father, and she is entering a similarly non-loving relationship with David.

Outwardly, Michal is in a privileged position. In a marriage in
which Michal loves her husband but David presumably fulfills his
conjugal duties without love, Michal may well confuse her social
worth and prestige with love. It is conceivable that Michal's sense of
her own worth is partially based on her position as daughter of the
king; she could well have convinced himself that this handsome shep-
herd/warrior is actually enamored of her.

Inwardly—daughter-as-object, daughter less important to her father
than revenge on a perceived enemy, daughter whose feelings are
totally ignored—Michal is probably not emotionally secure. These circumstances may contribute to Michal's loving David, a man socially
beneath her, as she seeks love and esteem from a man. Saul the king

---

5.   Adele Berlin attributes the 'notice that she loved David and that she made
it known' to Michal's 'unfeminine traits', and suggests that David 'expresses more
feelings of love and tenderness for the passive and submissive Jonathan than for
the aggressive and physical Michal'; Adele Berlin, 'Characterization in Biblical
Narrative: David's Wives', in David J.A. Clines and Tamara C. Eskenazi (eds.),
Telling Queen Michal's Story: An Experiment in Comparative Interpretation (JSOTSup,
119; Sheffield: Sheffield Academic Press, 1991), pp. 91-93. In view of David's devel-
oping history of relationships with women (e.g. Abigail, Bathsheba) and men (e.g.
Nabor, Uriah), Berlin's focus on gender in these relationships seems unwarranted.
David's preference is for individuals he can *control*: he apparently prefers docile
women—and men—to independent and resourceful ones.

has not shown Michal love; perhaps she thinks David the shepherd/warrior will show the king's daughter that love. Michal presumably does not know that David's pleasure is in being the king's son-in-law (1 Sam. 18.26) and not in being Michal's wife.

Instead of receiving validation from her loved one, Michal has, it seems, married a man much like her father. There is no indication that David has any regard for Michal. Significantly, in a society which regards woman's role as bearer of children, Michal has not conceived while married to David. All of these elements contribute to emotional shame. Nevertheless, Michal's conflict of inward shame and privileged life do not destroy her capacity to love. Her strength of character is indicated in that she does *not* continue in the victim role established with her father. Instead, Michal acts as rescuer of David in the triangulation with Saul: when Saul plots to kill his son-in-law, Michal assumes a rescuer role to save her victim husband—even though he is a warrior. She does not consult; she directs the action; and David silently complies. Saul persecutes David, Michal rescues David, thereby persecuting Saul. These actions show ambivalence in Michal's relationships with males.

When Michal protects David from her father's orders to his messengers to kill him, she 'let him down from the window' (1 Sam. 19.12), an effort which took rapid planning and possibly physical strength. Michal further postpones pursuit of David by putting *teraphim*, household idols, in bed in his place and even claiming that he is sick and can not appear to Saul's messengers (1 Sam. 19.14).

Saul insists that David be brought before him, in his sickbed if need be; when her ruse is exposed, Michal lies to her father to justify her actions (1 Sam. 19.17). In this demonstration of her allegiance, Michal 'chooses her husband over her father; this is an ironic anticipation of David's later rebuke to her that it was "the Lord who chose me rather than your father"' (2 Sam. 6.21).[6] On a practical level, Michal's lie permits her to remain safe from her father's wrath and possibly an integral part of the king's family (though as a married woman she belongs to her husband's family).[7] She acts resourcefully and admirably on behalf of her husband, but betrays her father—who has already betrayed her in his actions.

One way of interpreting this series of events is in terms of Michal's

6. Peter D. Miscall, 'Michal and her Sisters', in Clines and Eskenazi (eds.), *Telling Queen Michal's Story*, p. 250.

7. Zafrira Ben-Barak, 'The Legal Background to the Restoration of Michal to David', in Clines and Eskenazi (eds.), *Telling Queen Michal's Story*, pp. 74-90 (86).

self-sacrifice. One could also regard Michal's sending David away as a tacit recognition that her love for David has not been reciprocated. The household idols she places in her bed to deceive the king's messengers may be seen as symbolic representations of her husband's behavior in their relationship: images of wood or clay or stone or metal, unresponsive to the love Michal brought to the marriage. The reader knows David *is* capable of showing love. He has been affectionate, even kissing the passive, docile Jonathan (1 Sam. 20.41); the 'image' Michal puts in their bed suggests that David has been less than warm-blooded—more like something cold and inorganic—in his marriage bed. The idols in bed permit Michal-as-rescuer to gain more time for David, permit Michal-as-daughter to save herself, permit Michal-as-wife a retreat from denied intimacy. In this interpretation, Michal is not yet aware of David's refusal to commit himself; she is not yet admitting to herself the reality of his lack of interest in their marriage. She is sending away the man whom she still loves, protecting his life but not going with him.

It may be protested that Michal could not go with David, that she could not live the life of a highwayman's wife, but this assumes that David and Michal already know that he will live that life when he leaves the royal household. That assumption seems unlikely since David's departure is spontaneous—an immediate result of Michal's information about Saul's plans to have David killed that night.

Could David and Michal have gone to David's parents' home for safety? What other options were possible for a couple who wished to stay together? Abraham and Sarah travel great distances, as do other patriarchs and their wives. Although they are not escaping from their own hostile king, those couples do face other hostile forces, both within and outside their own families. It was not impossible for a woman to travel with her husband. But Michal tells David to save his life (1 Sam. 19.11) and sends David off alone. As a married woman, she is no longer technically a member of her father's household. Why does she choose to remain without her husband? Michal may be choosing to remain with a 'known' pain—her relationship with her father; she may be making a total sacrifice to save her husband; or at some (unconscious?) level, Michal may be acknowledging David's lack of interest in her.

Before Michal and David come into contact again, David has taken six additional wives and has fathered one son by each of them. Fewell and Gunn find that 'David's policy is to dissipate all power but his own. He will not have one wife but several. And no wife will be first in his house.'[8] Before Michal and David meet again, Saul gives his married daughter Michal to another man, 'Palti, son of Laish, who was from Gallim' (1 Sam. 25.44). [9] Inasmuch as this bit of information immediately follows the news of David's having taken two wives, the reader may infer that Saul considers it unlikely that the much-married David will still claim Michal as wife, or that Saul is expressing his hostility to David by 'killing' him symbolically with Michal's enforced 'widowhood'. Once again Michal is the victim. No mention is made of Michal's love of David, of her reaction to this turn of events or of her relationship to Palti.

After the death of Saul, a war between the House of Saul and the House of David develops, with Saul's followers in fragmented opposition to the increasingly powerful David. One follower, Abner, offers to make a pact with David, proposing to bring 'all Israel' to David's side as rebuke of Saul's son Ish-bosheth (2 Sam. 3.12). David's surprising response is to accept the pact with the singular demand of his 'wife, Michal, for whom I paid one hundred foreskins' (3.14). As her father 'gave' her to David and to Palti, once again Michal is transferred from male to male as an object.

To complicate matters, the reader learns that Michal's new husband Palti is deeply attached to her; although the text does not explicitly say so, it seems safe to assume that he loves her (3.12-16).[10] When Ish-bosheth and Abner take her from Palti to return her to her (first) husband, David, the focus is not on Michal but on Palti. The initiative Michal demonstrates when she sends David away is replaced by a passive Michal and a helpless husband who walks with her, weeping. In fact, Palti does not turn back from walking beside Michal until he is

8.   Danna Nolan Fewell and David M. Gunn, *Gender, Power & Promise: The Subject of the Bible's First Story* (Nashville: Abingdon Press, 1993), p. 157.

9.   Zafrira Ben-Barak has uncovered legal documentary material from Meso-potamia suggesting that when a husband is absent *against his will* for a period of two years, the wife—who is left without subsistence since she belongs to her hus-band's family—is declared a 'widow' and is entitled to remarry. Should the first husband return, the woman is obliged to return to him, but any children remain with their natural father. David is forced to flee for his life *against his will*, and Ben-Barak suggests that Saul's action in giving Michal to another man as wife is to be regarded as 'a customary official act and not as the arbitrary act of Saul giving his daughter in marriage'. Ben-Barak, 'The Legal Background', pp. 81-86, 88-89.

10.   Emotional attachment is entirely discounted by R.K. Harrison: 'The obvi-ous attachment of Phaltiel to Michal, as recorded in 2 Samuel 3.16, is again under-standable if she was in fact heiress to the throne, for in marrying her he would be in the direct line of succession' ('The Matriarchate and Hebrew Regal Succession', *EvQ* 29.1 [1957], pp. 29-34).

ordered to do so. Palti's devotion and helplessness provide a marked contrast to David, who has become decisive and aggressive since his wordless escape from Michal's window. The reader is pulled in two directions: by Palti's love for Michal and by recollections of Michal's love for David. The textual silence about Michal's feelings for Palti may encourage the reader to hope that the reunion with David will renew her love for him—or it may signal that Michal is as helpless as Palti and, possibly, even angry about being returned to the husband whom she remembers as unloving and 'wooden' in bed. The text is further silent about Michal's fruitfulness in her marriage to Palti. This silence may suggest that Michal has been infertile—that the impotent household idol she put in bed in place of David has indeed become symbolic of her lack of fecundity.

When David is king, he acts to bring the Ark of God to the City of David with great celebration, including sacrifices and dancing to the music of 'wood instruments, lyres, harps, timbrels, sistrums, and cymbals' (2 Sam. 6.5).[11] David himself, 'girt [only?] with a linen ephod', 'whirled with all his might' in dancing before the Lord (2 Sam. 6.14). The festivity of the shouts and blasts of the horn accompanying the progress of the awesome Ark is captured by the spectacle of the whirling, ecstatic king, a sight Michal catches from behind a window.

The contrast of this scene at the window with the earlier window scene is notable. In the earlier scene, Michal represents the royal family as daughter of Saul, and David is the powerless son-in-law. In the later scene, David *is* royalty—the king—and Michal is merely one of several wives. The window which provided David freedom and saved his life becomes a window which confines Michal, evidenced by the bitter tone of her words. The window 'frames' each of these scenes, much as it 'frames' David's earlier speechless passivity, and his later surge of uninhibited activity. The window also 'frames' the sexual content of each of the scenes: the marital bed with its representations of a powerless David as he leaves the first window scene, vis-à-vis the uninhibited, barely-covered David kicking up his legs and exposing his genitalia before the mixed-gender throng in the second window scene. The reader is invited to consider the developments in the lives of the protagonists through this literary 'window'.

In the conclusion of this passage (2 Sam. 6.20-23), King David

---

11. Although these musical instruments are explicitly mentioned only in the first phase of the journey, it is assumed that they also accompany the Ark in the second phase, from Obed-edom's house to the City of David, especially since David dances in the second phase.

distributes food to 'the entire multitude of Israel, man and woman alike' before the people leave for their homes (v. 19). One can well imagine the elation the king is enjoying when he returns to his own household. It is Michal who comes out to greet David upon his return—not with tambourines to welcome the returning hero but with caustic words. 'Didn't the king of Israel do himself honor today—exposing himself in the sight of the slavegirls of his subjects, as one of the riffraff might expose himself!' (v. 20). These words reveal an image of Michal entirely different from the one we encountered when Michal last spoke—the young woman resourcefully saving her husband's life even as she sends him away from her side. Interim events have apparently made Michal angry and sharp-tongued. Michal may regret her separation from Palti; she may feel that David is 'beneath her', as demonstrated by his exhibitionist behavior; she may resent the fact that she, who enjoyed the prestige of being the king's daughter, is merely one of several wives of this boorish king—and childless to boot. Michal's angry words to David suggest that she is displacing the shame she experiences in her situation on to David. David's response seizes on Michal's claim to royal breeding, but the narrator's commentary turns from the past to focus on the future: the text makes explicit that Michal remains childless:

'It was before the Lord who chose me instead of your father and all his family and appointed me ruler over the Lord's people Israel! I will dance before the Lord and dishonor myself even more, and be low in your[12] esteem; but among the slavegirls that you speak of I will be honored.'
And to her dying day Michal daughter of Saul had no children.

In his response, David defends himself passionately, indicating Michal's continuing importance to him at some level. His emotional retaliation reveals his own discomfort—shame? guilt?—through his emotional defensiveness.

Michal's voice is only heard in the initial and final phases of her life, so there is no possibility of determining precisely what effects the change from a loving and enthusiastic woman to a bitter harridan. It is clear that her father and her husband[13] have bandied her about like chattel, from 'man' to 'man'. But Michal has matured. Saul is now dead, and Michal is no longer in denial about her relationship with David. Freed of her father's abuse, Michal finally owns her own

12. This is the Septuagint reading. The Masoretic Text reads 'my own'.
13. Excluding Palti as a husband, since that marriage was effectively annulled by her being returned to David, her first husband

power by confronting David, by becoming a person, not an object. She regains her voice, but she remains childless.

It may be that David recalled Michal as wife to ensure that no off-spring of Saul would threaten his line of succession. The text does leave open the remote possibility that Michal herself refuses to give David children: notice of her childlessness immediately follows David's remarks with an opening conjunction, 'and', thus avoiding attributing, but not denying, any relationship between David's repu-diation of Michal and her childlessness.[14] It is more likely that the text punishes Michal for her haughty words, which seem to ensure that David will not visit her bed and that Michal's childlessness is her punishment for speaking out against YHWH's anointed. In this read-ing, it is David, not Michal's own barrenness, who renders her child-less. Michal has apparently never been pregnant, but David's implied reaction obviates the possibility of Michal's being a 'late bloomer' like Sarah, Rebecca and Hannah.

Even if David would visit her bed, the fact is that Michal is not in control of her capacity to reproduce. J. Cheryl Exum has suggested that 'Since it is YHWH who opens and closes the womb (Gen. 20.18; 29.31; 30.2, 22; 1 Sam. 1.5, 6; Isa. 66.9), perhaps the deity bears respon-sibility'.[15] I propose the text subtly places the source of Michal's barrenness on Michal herself, symbolized by her putting household idols in her bed.

The text indicates that as a young woman Michal had, and may have worshipped, idols. Her putting the idols in her bed to take the place of the fleeing David carries a wealth of meaning: a clever ruse to give David time to flee, a symbol of David's relationship to Michal, and an exposure of her failure to worship the one God of the Israel-ites. A household idol is, after all, an image of a foreign god. As Peter Miscall observes, 'Worship of foreign gods is the main snare, *moqesh*, in the narrative in Genesis–2 Kings'.[16]

Since it is God who determines women's capacity to bear children in biblical texts, who remembers barren women and allows them to

---

14. Robert Alter bemoans 'modern translators [who] generally destroy the fineness of the effect of rendering the initial "and" as "so"', thus establishing an unambiguous causal connection. 'Characterization and the Art of Reticence', in Clines and Eskenazi (eds.), *Telling Queen Michal's Story*, pp. 64-73 (73).

15. J. Cheryl Exum, 'Murder They Wrote: Ideology and the Manipulation of Female Presence in Biblical Narrative', in Clines and Eskenazi (eds.), *Telling Queen Michal's Story*, pp. 176-98 (185).

16. Miscall, 'Michal and her Sisters', p. 250 n. 1.

become pregnant, it seems likely that God would not remember Michal. We recall that Rachel, whom God remembered after many years of infertility (Gen. 30.22), was punished after she stole her father's household idols—and they were not her own. Furthermore, when Jacob demands that all the 'foreign gods' in the camp be brought to him for burial and purification before proceeding to Bethel (Gen. 35.2-4), it is assumed that Rachel also relinquishes the idols she brought with her. In this delicate balance of fertility and faith, Rachel bears another son but dies at his birth.

Michal, however, is never shown to relinquish the idols she has available to put in her bed. Furthermore, Michal's ridiculing of David's ecstatic abandon depicts her as more interested in the propriety of royal behavior than joy in the one God. Michal is a barren wife, I suggest, because she has been portrayed as barren of belief in the God of Israel, the God who could open her womb. Thus God can be included among the males who persecute Michal. As a later text compares the works of God with those of idols (Judg. 10.13), this text suggests that if Michal puts idols in her bed, let the idols make her pregnant. Michal is childless because she is depicted not as a God-fearing woman but as a woman who values her household gods and her royal status, a woman who presumes to think and act for herself, flying in the face of tradition rather than demurely moderating her social position and personal capacities. She is a loving and nurturing woman and a victim of male egocentricity. The author(s) of this text presents a complex portrait of Michal, one that evokes sympathy even as it condemns.

The first re-telling of these events (1 Chron. 15.29) focuses on David rather than Michal, paraphrasing only 2 Sam. 16.16. Without the additional information provided in the books of Samuel, this one verse uses Michal, daughter of Saul, to highlight David's greatness. Rabbinic literature, however, is not so dismissive. In her valuable article, 'Michal in Hebrew Sources', Tamara Eskenazi finds that 'the rabbis generally praise her and sympathize not only with her but also with her second husband Palti'.[17] Eskenazi also offers modern midrashic responses to Michal—which may portray her as a heroine or as a victim—and recent scholarly responses.[18] 'As a compassionate sister, as romantic heroine or as a tragic victim, Michal in Hebrew literature

---

17. Tamara C. Eskenazi, 'Michal in Hebrew Sources', in Clines and Eskenazi (eds.), *Telling Queen Michal's Story*, pp. 156-74. Quotation on p. 158.

18. Eskenazi, 'Michal in Hebrew Sources', pp. 159-74.

is more often praised than blamed.'[19] But each of these views is partial and thereby diminishes Michal's story.

Even though this narrative sequence is full of irresolvable gaps, Michal deserves to be accorded the complexity of her portrayal in the books of Samuel. She is depicted as a woman who has the capacity for love and nurturing, as evidenced by her early exchange with David; and as a woman reduced to a life of pain and ultimate oblivion by power-hungry men and an omnipotent and unforgiving God. The saving grace of the men in her life is that they did not have, and probably did not worship, idols, whereas Michal apparently did. Readers have long accepted the flawed male protagonists of the Hebrew Bible. Michal serves as a female counterweight, denied a significant role because her flaw involves denial of the God of Israel. The male-dominated religious culture and its authors sacrificed Michal's admirable qualities to Saul's and David's self-aggrandizing ones. The punishment accorded her is the most harsh and unjust the biblical writers could wreak: her story depicts a woman's degradation from love and joy into a life of pain and shame, and suffering the worst insult of all: the failure of the one purpose in life that biblical women could aspire to achieve, motherhood and descendants.

Michal is yet another imperfect human being in the Hebrew Bible. As such, she deserves more than glorification or victimization. She deserves the full complex difficulty of her story.

19. Eskenazi, 'Michal in Hebrew Sources', p. 173.

BATHSHEBA REVEALED

Lillian R. Klein

Although she is the mother of Solomon, regarded in the Hebrew Bible and in some critical traditions as the greatest monarch of the Israelite people, Bathsheba is relatively neglected in commentary. She is not mentioned (except as the object of David's desire) in a study on the monarchic period, even when the subject is the 'Matriarchate and Hebrew Regal Succession'.[1] Adele Berlin views Bathsheba in her introductory appearance as 'a complete non-person. She is not even a minor character, but simply part of the plot'.[2] Commentators take little note of Bathsheba's feelings—or David's—'despite the fact that powerful and deep emotions play a crucial role' in the seduction scene (2 Sam. 11).[3] In sum, Bathsheba as an individual, as a woman, scarcely exists in the Hebrew Bible and in biblical interpretation, and even then almost exclusively through the lens of male perception.

It is male perception that introduces Bathsheba and the central plot conflict (2 Sam. 11): David sees her bathing as he walks on the roof of the palace in the evening. He sends for her, and she becomes pregnant by him as a result of one sexual encounter—while still married to another man. Her husband Uriah, a Hittite soldier in the king's army, is away at war, which presents a delicate situation.

---

1. R.K. Harrison, 'The Matriarchate and Hebrew Regal Succession', *EvQ* 29.1 (1957), pp. 29-34. Harrison focuses on the possible influence women in the line of descent might have had in struggles for accession to the throne. Because Bathsheba, though of high birth, was not among the royal line of descent, she is not mentioned as matriarch. See also Tomoo Ishida, *The Royal Dynasties in Ancient Israel: A Study on the Formation and Development of Royal-Dynastic Ideology* (Berlin: W. de Gruyter, 1977); J.D. Levenson and B. Halpern, 'The Political Import of David's Marriages', *JBL* 99.4 (1980), pp. 507- 18.

2. Adele Berlin, *Poetics and Interpretation of Biblical Narrative* (Bible and Literature Series; Sheffield: Almond Press, 1983), p. 27.

3. Shimon Bar-Efrat, *Narrative Art in the Bible* (JSOTSup, 70; Sheffield: Almond Press, 1989), pp. 22-23. See earlier comments by David M. Gunn, who considers the absence of emotional content in the story (*The Story of King David: Genre and Interpretation* [JSOTSup, 5; Sheffield, JSOT Press, 1982], p. 99).

The text is ambiguous about Bathsheba's role: in commentary, she is generally polarized as either a temptress, bathing on her roof to catch David's attention,[4] or as an innocent victim of David's lust.[5] Mieke Bal suggests that ironic ambiguity 'prevents the reader from making more specific interpretations'.[6] Provocatively, the text does not hold Bathsheba accountable for the adultery, while blame is heaped on David.[7]

While the seduction scene is meager (and the child of lust dies), it does eventuate in Bathsheba's becoming the mother of a king; and she is the third woman identified as a mother to royal lineage in biblical texts. Tamar (Gen. 38.13-26) and Ruth are identified as ancestral mothers-of-kings, and their stories suggest parallels which amplify the little we know about Bathsheba.[8]

The Gap in the Text

Bathsheba is first seen as an object—a beautiful woman who is bathing. An unknown 'someone' in David's court identifies her to David

4.   Menachem Perry and Meir Sternberg, 'The King through Ironic Eyes: The Narrator's Devices in the Story of David and Bathsheba and Two Excursuses on the Theory of the Narrative Text', *Hasifrut* 1 (1968). Published as 'Gaps, Ambiguity and the Reading Process', in Meir Sternberg (ed.), *The Poetics of Biblical Narrative: Ideological Literature and the Drama of Reading* (Bloomington: Indiana University Press, 1985), pp. 186-229 (201-204) (page reference to this edition); Randall C. Bailey, *David in Love and War: The Pursuit of Power in 2 Samuel 10–12* (JSOTSup, 75; Sheffield: Sheffield Academic Press, 1990), p. 89.

5.   J.P. Fokkelman, *Narrative Art and Poetry in the Books of Samuel: A Full Interpretation Based on Stylistic and Structural Analyses* (2 vols.; Assen: Van Gorcum, 1981), I, p. 53; discussed by Mieke Bal, *Lethal Love: Feminist Literary Readings of Biblical Love Stories* (Bloomington: Indiana University Press, 1987), pp. 25-29. Gail A. Yee discusses both sides in 'Fraught with Background: Literary Ambiguity in II Samuel 11', *Int* 42.3 (July 1988), pp. 240-53 (243).

6.   Bal, *Lethal Love*, p. 23.

7.   Fokkelman, 'The text is moreover not at all interested in her possibly having shared the responsibility' (*Narrative Art*, p. 53); Bal, 'Anxiety about possible adultery seems to go against respect for the victimized woman' (*Lethal Love*, p. 28).

8.   I am not claiming the title of 'Queen-mother' for Bathsheba although she has been called the first *G^ebîrâ* and the paradigm for the senior status of the queen mother. For the pro-Queen mother, see R.N. Whybray, *The Succession Narrative: A Study of 11 Samuel 9–2 and 1 Kings 1 and 2* (SBT, 2.9; London: SCM Press, 1968), p. 40; Ishida, *Royal Dynasties*, pp. 142, 155-58. For a very convincing argument against, see Zafrira Ben-Barak, 'The Status and Right of the *G^ebîrâ*', in Athalya Brenner (ed.), *A Feminist Companion to Samuel and Kings* (Feminist Companion to the Bible, 5; Sheffield: Sheffield Academic Press, 1994), pp. 170-85.

through her male relationships (father and husband). Bathsheba the individual is recognized as pedigreed (of an important family), beautiful and bathing. Her bathing—purifying herself, as Meir Sternberg has made us aware—indicates she has completed her menses and, therefore, is not pregnant.[9] We note that Bathsheba is bathing in the evening, when she could be seen, rather than in the obscurity of the night.

In this scene, David's association with active verbs, particularly his repeated exercise of שלח, 'send', marks his command of the situation. Bathsheba, though she is the object of male actions—she 'is taken' (from לקח) by the servant and David lays with her—is not utterly passive; she 'comes' (from בוא) to David.[10] Noting that Bathsheba's arrival and sexual involvement are fully covered without the phrase, 'and she came to him', the reader is alerted to excess verbiage, bordering on redundancy, which demands attention. The superfluous words do serve to mitigate Bathsheba's passivity, to be sure; and the use of 'come', with its connotations of sexuality, insinuates Bathsheba's complicity in the sexual adventure. From Bathsheba's point-of-view, her complicity with the king's wishes may be regarded as her attempt to bear a child rather than merely participation in an adulterous (lustful) act.

The end of the encounter mentions purification by Bathsheba once again:

> And David sent messengers and took her and she came to him and he lay with her and she purified herself from her uncleanness and she returned to her house (2 Sam. 11.4; literal translation).

Bathsheba's purification at this juncture is usually interpreted as referring to her earlier purification:

> David sent messengers to fetch her; she came to him and he lay with her—she had just purified herself after her period—and she went back home (JPS).

> So David sent messengers, and took her; and she came to him, and he lay with her. (Now she was purifying herself from her uncleanness.) (Oxford).

---

9. Sternberg, 'Gaps, Ambiguity'.

10. Randall Bailey observes that Bathsheba's 'actions are not in the hiph'il verb forms, which would suggest that she was being "caused to act". Rather they are in the qal, she comes and returns…a willing and equal partner to the events which transpire' (Bailey, *David in Love and War*, p. 88).

Two words are critical: 'purified' and 'uncleanness'. The Hebrew מתקדשת is the hith. participle (singular, feminine) of קדשׁ; extending the meaning to 'set apart', it denotes 'to consecrate oneself by purification, of priests and Levites, and of woman'.[11] The second word, מטמאתה, 'from her uncleanness' from טמאה, 'uncleanness', usually refers to sexual or to ethical and religious uncleanness. These encompass a range of ritual uncleanness of men and women's uncleanness resulting from copulation and menstruation.[12] There is just one narrative instance of 'ritual uncleanness' of woman: that of Bathsheba, in this verse. The initial reference to Bathsheba's purifying herself does not mention her 'uncleanness'; it states only that she is bathing. Although v. 4 can be interpreted as referring to her earlier purification from her menses, it seems an awkward reading. I suggest Bathsheba's second purification may be from her sexual and ethical uncleanness. In any case, whether this purification is understood to reiterate Bathsheba's earlier ritual or to reflect her purifying herself a second time, after the sexual act, the sexual act *concludes* with emphasis on Bathsheba's *purification*. In this reading, the repetition of 'purification' at this juncture in the text hints at Bathsheba's motive—not desire for a sexual romp but desire for motherhood. With 'purification', her complicity is absolved from unethical behavior. This reading justifies Bathsheba's vindication in the text and subsequent commentary.

Bathsheba has no voice before or during the sexual encounter. David's voice, while not quoted directly, is conveyed through the mission he directs: He *sends* someone to inquire; he *sends* messengers to get her. Only when her body has 'spoken' does Bathsheba demonstrate command of the situation. The sudden burst of four verbs associated with Bathsheba contrasts with her earlier docile silence. Her first action is *conception*: her body acts. The conception gives her power to send, as previously David repeatedly *sent*: Bathsheba acts. With sending, she has voice and *speaks*. Bathsheba's two words constitute the first direct speech in the narrative, and her words are directed to the king. To this point, David has spoken only indirectly, but Bathsheba tells; she speaks directly.[13] Finally, Bathsheba's speaking is emphasized with yet another reference to speech: her speech is announced when she 'says' to David, 'I [am] pregnant' (11.5).

11. BDB, p. 873b.
12. Ritual uncleanness of males: Lev. 5.3; 7.20, 21; 14.19; 15.3-11, 16-17, 24; Num. 19.13; Lev. 22.3, 5; of females: Lev. 5.18-23; 25-30.
13. The mode of speech may convey an ethical quality even though both David and Bathsheba have knowingly committed adultery.

This sequence suggests that conception gives woman power, perhaps power beyond that of the male. Woman's body can speak and
give woman speech.[14] Furthermore, the woman's speech initiates
male response. David's authority, with repeated verbs of action—
sending people here and there—is subtly undermined by the woman,
for the balance of action in the narrative is in response to Bathsheba's
two words of direct speech: 'I [am] pregnant'. Of course Bathsheba's
words are the result of David's sending for her; but if, as I suggest,
Bathsheba is complicit in the sexual encounter, she is less the object
than is readily apparent.

Although the reader cannot discern the tone of Bathsheba's words,
they are baldly direct: there is no hedging or apology or humble
appeal to the king. These are not the words of an intimidated woman,
although we are to suppose her seduction by the king involves intim-
idation. The king does not entice Bathsheba with seductive words; he
'sends' for her and 'takes' her. David's actions presume the privileges
of power, which depend upon subordinates being intimidated by
that power. It is possible that Bathsheba is initially intimidated but
becomes self-confident once she acquires the power of pregnancy.
Another possibility, which does not invoke this dramatic change of
personality, is that Bathsheba has not been intimidated at any point. If
Bathsheba is not intimidated, has Bathsheba been 'taken', or has
David?

Bathsheba's words are the only words of direct speech by either of
the main characters to one another until David is old and approaching
death. David speaks indirectly to a nameless 'someone' and sends
nameless messengers, actions which may be perceived as symbolic of
David's indirect, unethical actions. Ironically, David later speaks
directly to Bathsheba's husband, urging him to go home and wash his
feet.[15] He also sends a 'gift' after Uriah.[16] David's intention is clearly
that Uriah sleep with his wife Bathsheba and relieve David of a
difficult situation.

But Uriah does not go home. He lies down at the entrance of the
king's house. Uriah 'lay', וישכב, alone, exactly as David 'lay', וישכב,

---

14. J. Cheryl Exum, 'Bathsheba's Body "Speaks" in an Obvious Way, Giving
Her Voice', in *Fragmented Women: Feminist (Sub)versions of Biblical Narratives* (Valley
Forge, PA: Trinity Press, 1993), p. 190.

15. 'Feet' are a well-know euphemism for sexual organs.

16. The words chosen to convey 'gift' is derived from נשא (in niph) 'be carried,
be married, be lifted': '...and the king sent after Uriah an exaltation, a marriage
from the king'.

with Bathsheba earlier—but Uriah's action ironically *opposes* the king's wishes. Both Bathsheba and Uriah respond to the king's orders in a manner overtly passive but in fact active: Bathsheba acquiesces to orders she may herself have precipitated; Uriah resists. Uriah's refusal suggests it is not necessary to accede to the king's orders—at least for a man. It may be another question as to whether a woman can refuse the king—if she wants to—even if the order is sexual and immoral.[17]

The text has led the reader to surmise that Bathsheba is not pregnant when she sleeps with David; since no mention is made of children, it may be assumed that she has never conceived. No hint is offered as to how long Bathsheba has been a married woman, without conception; yet she conceives as a result of one sexual encounter with David. Typically, biblical narratives assume the problem with failure to conceive is that of the woman; I know of no narrative text that even acknowledges the possibility of male infertility. Sarah, Hannah, Rachel all conceive after long periods of infertility—with the help of (a male) God; and each of those narratives supports the fact of male fertility (hence female infertility) with a secondary woman who becomes pregnant by the same husband. It seems that male sterility among the Israelites is not to be countenanced. However, it is possible that Bathsheba's husband may implicitly be permitted infertility since he is, after all, a Hittite. Faithful as he is to the Israelites, his patrimony is different. Perhaps, in this narrative, not all males of other races are as virile as the Israelites.[18]

David's object in the liaison is clear: lust.[19] Bathsheba, however, may not be only the passive object of his lust.[20] If she has been married to an infertile man, warrior though he is, she may find it necessary to mate with another male to fulfill her biological and social function as a woman—to become a mother. Granted, she may not have known where the infertility lay—with her or her husband—but her failure to conceive is no doubt of great concern to her. As a married woman, she cannot test her capacity for reproduction outside of

17. When the servants tell David that Uriah did not go down to his house, no mention is made of the 'gift', and the verb is not 'come', but 'go', without sexual implications.

18. In other biblical texts (Ezek. 16; Jer. 5; Deut. and more) foreign males are sexually active and fertile.

19. Randall Bailey views this as a story 'of political intrigue in which sex becomes a tool of politics' (Bailey, *David in Love and War*, p. 88).

20. Bailey: '...the narrator suggests that she is here as well as throughout the narrative a willing and equal partner to the events which transpire' (*David in Love and War*, p. 88).

her marital bonds; but if the king commands her, she has the pretext of excuse. Bathsheba can accept the king's order and at the same time fulfill her mission: to bear sons.

Provocatively, the text leaves ambiguous the circumstances of Bathsheba's ritual bathing. Has Bathsheba regularly bathed on her roof? In this scenario, David may be aware of the beautiful woman whose husband is now in the field, and David makes his move. Or is this the first time Bathsheba has bathed on the roof, potentially in view of the king? In this perspective, she has chosen to purify herself there now, when her husband is in the field and she is again not pregnant. The text does not suggest that David's walking on his roof was motivated by any ulterior motives; on the contrary, David's spontaneity—in walking and seeing and taking—reinforces Bathsheba's maneuver in bathing on her roof *at this time*. I suggest Bathsheba may well have been purifying herself on her roof with the hope of seducing King David into 'seducing' her.

In this light, Bathsheba may knowingly 'come' to the king in the hope of conceiving without renouncing her honor. In the social context of this narrative, women usually achieve honor by preserving their positive 'shame'—by deference and submission to male authority—and by the status accorded motherhood. In this reading, Bathsheba seeks the honor associated with motherhood instead of accepting its opposite, social discrimination as a barren woman. She risks a single 'shameless' incident of sexual infidelity—forbidden for women—in order to achieve lasting honor as a mother.[21] But Bathsheba avoids the sexual autonomy forbidden women. She acts in deference and submission to male authority. Bathsheba's purification before—and especially after—the act reinforces the ethical aspect of the encounter for her. Female-initiated seduction (viz. Ruth) or adultery (see Tamar [Gen. 38.13-26]) may be textually regarded as righteous if the action answers to a good cause—and for a biblical woman, that cause is procreation.[22] Bathsheba continues the paradigm estab-

21. For a fuller discussion of this concept, see my 'Honor and Shame in Esther', in Athalya Brenner (ed.), *A Feminist Companion to Esther, Judith and Susanna* (Feminist Companion to the Bible, 7; Sheffield: Sheffield Academic Press, 1995), pp. 149-75.

22. Of course Bathsheba's pregnancy does create a dilemma. Her husband's absence when she becomes pregnant underscores her fertility and his unfertility, which further heightens the tension. Bathsheba not only cuckolds her husband but makes his infertility—his lack of manhood—public. How characteristic that a male who cannot fulfill the essential masculine role, to fertilize, devotes himself to a militaristic career—as it were to prove his manhood.

lished by her female predecessors: women as mothers in the royal lineage.

Woman as Mother

> Childbearing was a social function in ancient Israel, and fecundity, barrenness, and the loss of children were of urgent concern to men, women, and the nation.[23]

I propose that Bathsheba's desire for motherhood causes her to exploit her sexual allure as a temptress in order to gain her objective, which involves adultery with the king; yet her actions are excused by the implied narrator. Significantly, Bathsheba is never considered a temptress by biblical commentators; 'the temptress in biblical literature is a figure of the strange, alien, shadowy "other" in which one may lose one's bearings, one's sense of order'.[24] Bathsheba is not 'other'—she is descended from an important Israelite family but she does cause David to lose his bearings. A temptress, furthermore, 'portrays one who mediates a destiny contrary to the divine purpose', and Bathsheba's desire to become a mother, in this reading, is utterly consistent with the divine purpose.[25] In any case, 'biblical stories do not draw up an absolute, clear-cut line of separation between the temptress and Israel's heroines'.[26] Bathsheba presents a subtle opportunity for enticement rather than an overt sexual invitation.

Phyllis Bird observes that 'The two most common images of woman in the historical writings are those of wife and mother',[27] yet there was a gulf between these two roles. The wife as such was almost invisible; the wife who was childless (presumed barren) was a reproach in Israel: she was derided by other women, her role as wife was threatened, and she was denied the honor identified with being a mother. Motherhood offered the highest status for women and, more than honor, it brought security through the approval of husband and community. Motherhood also 'offered the woman her only opportunity to exercise legitimate power over another person... The only relation-

23. John Otwell, *And Sarah Laughed: The Status of Woman in the Old Testament* (Philadelphia: Westminster Press, 1977), Chapter 4: 'Woman as Mother', p. 50.

24. James G. Williams, *Women Recounted: Narrative Thinking and the God of Israel* (Sheffield: Almond Press, 1982), p. 92.

25. Williams, *Women Recounted*, p. 107.

26. Williams, *Women Recounted*, p. 92.

27. Phyllis A. Bird, 'Images of Women in the Old Testament', in Norman K. Gottwald (ed.), *The Bible and Liberation: Political and Social Hermeneutics* (Maryknoll, NY: Orbis Books, 1983), pp. 252-88 (268).

ship in which dominance by the woman was sanctioned was the mother–child relationship'.[28] For Bathsheba, motherhood, especially with the king as father to her child, is a means for advancing her standing in the community. Bathsheba's purpose—motherhood—and the divine orders to humans—generation—are one and the same.

Paradigm as Gap-Replenisher

This reading of Bathsheba's actions offers interesting correspondences with those of her predecessors as foremothers in the Davidic lineage: the very same Tamar and Ruth alluded to earlier. Significantly, all three tales of female predecessors of kings are highly sexual in content and exhibit women as initiators of sexual encounters. Tamar (Gen. 38.13-26), we recall, seduces her father-in-law by presenting herself as a veiled prostitute in order to conceive when Judah's youngest son has been withheld from her. Ruth, childless and widowed, uncovers Boaz's feet on the threshing floor; and he understands her intent (3.1-14). Bathsheba bathes where she is visible from the roof of the king's house, a favorite place to walk in the evening (2 Sam. 11.2) All these female ancestors/mothers of kings know they want motherhood, and they take action to make sure they conceive. To do so, they use their beauty to arouse the sexual desire that excites males: they make themselves the object of male desire but exhibit no sexual desire themselves.

These encounters may involve deception, as Tamar disguises herself as a prostitute (Gen. 38.12-19); and Ruth steals into the threshing floor under the cloak of darkness, when Boaz is asleep, to lie down at his feet (Ruth 3.1-14). In a biblical twist, Bathsheba's story turns the deception from the female to the male, to David, who attempts to foist Bathsheba's pregnancy off on Uriah. Deception in the realization of divine purpose (propagation of the people) is not judged harshly; in contrast, David's deception (and subsequent murder) of Uriah is condemned and punished.

Two of the three ancestresses/mothers-of-kings take an exterior memento of the occasion. Tamar takes Judah's staff and signet (Gen. 38.17-18), and Ruth takes an apron full of grain home to Naomi (Ruth 3.15). Bathsheba takes only the seed in her body away from the encounter. She does not defend her actions (by identifying the accuser as the perpetrator) as Tamar does, and she is not responsible as a

---

28. Bird, 'Images of Women in the Old Testament', p. 269.

daughter (like Ruth). Bathsheba acts as an independent agent and has no memento except what she sought: conception.

Interestingly, each of these unusual alliances involves a third party in the behind-the-scenes arrangements. Judah seeks to redeem his pledge by sending the promised kid with his friend the Adullamite (Gen. 38.20) Ruth is sent to the threshing-floor by Naomi (Ruth 3.1-5); and Bathsheba is identified by 'someone' and brought to the king by 'messengers' (2 Sam. 11.3). Actions, casual or not, may become significant as events unfold, and they are witnessed.

The goal of each of the ancestresses/mothers-of-kings is presumed to include conception. Tamar certainly wishes to conceive in the line of Judah. Ruth, widowed without children, obeys Naomi's wish that she marry, with conception implicit; and Bathsheba, childless, may be presumed to desire conception. Furthermore, two of these three women conceive from a single sexual encounter. Tamar conceives twins by Judah, and Bathsheba bears a son.[29] Ruth's conception is not attributed to her meeting with Boaz on the threshing floor, but the text suggests that she conceives without any delay (Ruth 4.13). These narratives portray ancestresses of kings as highly fertile.

Intertextual reading suggests that both Tamar's and Ruth's initiation of the sexual act subtly reinforces Bathsheba's active role in her sexual encounter with David. Furthermore, like her forbears as mothers of royal lineage, Bathsheba is determined to fulfill her role as a woman, even by unorthodox means.

The repeated motif of female sexual initiative in female progenitors of kings suggests this is an acceptable quality in a woman who is determined to bear children—sons, of course, in this male-dominated perspective. Significantly, these women are beautiful. James Williams observes that 'The arche-mother's beauty is a code communicating that she is blessed and that her progeny will be favored. This seems to work out almost without exception for biblical persons.'[30] They are also not driven by lust. Thus ancestresses/mothers of kings are both

29. The son of this conception dies, but Bathsheba and David conceive a second son, Solomon, who becomes heir to the throne.

30. Williams, *Women Recounted*, p. 47. Peter Miscall observes that David's male beauty 'serves no obvious function in this story, although there are allusions to it in 1 Sam 16:12 and 1 Sam 17:42' (Peter D. Miscall, *1 Samuel: A Literary Reading* [Bloomington: Indiana University Press, 1986], p. 119); David Gunn suggests female beauty 'usually communicates their sexual desirability in stories of courtship, seduction or rape' and that 'David's and Absalom's appearance perhaps related directly to their ability to charm' (David M. Gunn and Danna Nolan Fewell, *Narrative in the Hebrew Bible* [Oxford: Oxford University Press, 1993], p. 57).

desirable to their husbands (beautiful) and safe as wives (not likely to be unfaithful).

These narrative patterns suggest type-actions associated with mothers-of-kings, depicted in Table 1.

Table 1. *Bathsheba: Female Progenitor of a King*

Motif	Tamar	Ruth	Bathsheba
Narrative quite sexual	X	X	X
Woman makes herself object of male desire	X	X	X
Encounter involves deception	X	X	X
Third party privy to encounter	X	X	X
Woman takes memento of occasion	X	X	X
Woman's goal is/may be conception	X	X	X
Woman conceives from single encounter	X	?	X
Child in direct line to/is future king	X	X	X
Woman's narrative ends with birth of son(s)	X	X	—

Unlike these female royal precursors, earlier women—Sarah and Rachel, for example—turn to other women's fertility to supplant their own when they do not conceive. They doubt their fertility. In contrast, Tamar, Ruth and Bathsheba act as if they *know* they are capable of conception, and they find some means to realize their potential as woman, as mother. The story of Hannah, in 1 Sam. 1.1, provides an interesting intermediary link. As in earlier narratives, another woman bears her husband's children, but not at Hannah's suggestion. Like the mothers of royal lineage, Hannah insists on her own conception; however, her conception takes place in response to prayer and is thus precipitated by God, not by her own initiative.

The ancestresses/mothers of kings, like other narrative women, are depicted as having one social function: breeding. However, these women know what they want and they take steps to get their desires by all means. Where legitimacy is equivocal, they purify themselves (Bathsheba), receive blessings (Ruth), or prove their rights (Tamar).[31]

31. Of these 'royal' women, Bathsheba and Tamar execute their plans as inde-

There is one dramatic difference between the Tamar/Ruth and Bath-sheba narratives. The stories of the earlier women end with the birth of their sons, but Bathsheba continues to play an active role in the narrative; in fact, the narrative develops her individuality and strength as a king's mother. Alice Bach, comparing David's wives, observes: 'Only Bathsheba, the wife of sexual intimacy, participates in the on-going story of David's reign. The length of female textual life seems to be directly connected to the extent of sexual pleasure she provides her male creators.'[32]

Bathsheba is not mentioned in the sickness and death of the son of adultery, though David's response is narrated in detail (2 Sam. 12.15-23). After the infant's death, however, David 'comforts' his wife Bath-sheba, implying his recognition of her grief even as he validates her concern with motherhood. Bathsheba's second conception is thus not initiated merely by lust but, perhaps, by both compassion and sexual desire. Implicitly, the offspring of compassion and desire is more suitable to becoming a king than the product of casual carnal lust.

Bathsheba and Nathan

When King David is old, his political frailty is depicted through sexual impotence (1 Kgs 1.1-4).[33] Even a beautiful young maiden cannot warm him; she nurses him but 'the king knew her not' and Abishag the Shunammite remains a virgin.[34] The political implica-tions are immediately apparent as Adonijah seeks to usurp the throne. The frailty of David is also implicitly contrasted with the continuing vitality of Bathsheba and all the other characters presented.

It is Nathan, initially vehemently opposed to David's conduct in the Bathsheba affair,[35] who advises Bathsheba of Adonijah's actions to

pendent agents whereas Ruth works in concert with another woman to execute her plan.

32.   Alice Bach, 'The Pleasure of her Text', in Athalya Brenner (ed.), *A Feminist Companion to Samuel and Kings* (A Feminist Companion to the Bible, 5; Sheffield: Sheffield Academic Press, 1994), pp. 106-128 (122).

33.   'The hint of sexual impotence establishes the tone of the political scene to follow' (David M. Gunn, *The Story of King David: Genre and Interpretation* [JSOTSup, 6; Sheffield: University of Sheffield Press, 1978], p. 90).

34.   'With the father barely dead, his two sons [quarrel] over his bed-fellow—clearly no impotence theirs! (Gunn, *Story*, p. 90).

35.   'Nathan does not concentrate on the erotic part of David's crime, possibly because for him the appropriation of a woman, and even a married one, might have been recognized (if not necessarily approved of) as a royal prerogative. He

secure the kingship and how she must act to save her life and that of her son Solomon.[36] Nathan tells Bathsheba exactly what to say to the king: essentially, Bathsheba is to remind David of his vow that Solomon shall reign after him. Nathan promises he will come in after her and confirm her words. This scene is striking not only because of Nathan's sudden concord with Bathsheba, but also because this cooperation sounds like a conspiracy. Nathan's promise to confirm Bathsheba's words instills the idea that her words *need* verification: that they may not be not true, that there possibly was no earlier vow. According to this reading, Nathan and Bathsheba are joining forces to ensure that Bathsheba's son becomes king, despite Adonijah's legitimate claim to succession as the elder son.

As charged by Nathan, Bathsheba goes to the king's chamber—which presumes some special standing and suggests Nathan's awareness of her privileges in choosing to approach David through her. With Bathsheba's appearance before David, the reader is once more reminded of the king's age and frailty; he is apparently limited to bed to conduct even political matters. Bathsheba finds 'Abishag the Shunammite ministering to the king' but ignores the maiden: 'She bowed and did obeisance to the king' (1 Kgs 1.15). The mention of Abishag's presence and Bathsheba's inattention to her suggests some tension between the women and could imply Bathsheba's resentment of the younger woman. In any case, this wordless encounter effectively reverses the secondary-woman role of earlier narratives: instead of being the mother of children while the primary wife is barren, this secondary woman cannot even arouse the husband to intercourse, let along become pregnant. Bathsheba's aloofness also suggests her self-assurance and command of the situation. In contrast, David's weakness is reinforced by his brief, two-word reply to Bathsheba's homage.

She responds with a surprisingly vigorous speech. Bathsheba has seemed passive as she follows Nathan's counsel without a word in response to his directives, but her speech to David reveals her as assertive, expressing Nathan's ideas but with much more vigor than he suggests. (In the following citations, different fonts identify Bath-

does say, "I [the Lord] gave you his [Saul's] kingdom and his wives" (2 Sam. 12.8); nevertheless, this is of less weight in comparison to the moral crime committed against Uriah'. Shulamit Valler, 'King David and "His" Women: Biblical Stories and Talmudic Discussions', in Brenner (ed.), *Feminist Companion to Samuel and Kings*, pp. 129-42 (140).

36. Adonijah invited 'all his brothers, the king's sons, and all the royal officials of Judah, but he did not invite Nathan the prophet or Benaiah or the mighty men or Solomon his brother' (1 Kgs 9b).

sheba's verbatim repetition of Nathan's words, her additions, and her
change of verb tenses.)
  Nathan's version:

> Did you not, O lord king, swear to your maidservant: 'Your son
> Solomon shall succeed me as king, and he shall sit upon my throne?
> Why then has Adonijah become king?' (1 Kgs 1.13; JPS).

Bathsheba's version:

> 'My lord, you yourself **swore** to your maidservant *by the Lord your God*:
> Your son Solomon shall succeed me as king, and he shall sit upon my
> throne.' *Yet now* Adonijah has become king, *and you, my lord the king,
> know nothing about it. He has prepared a sacrificial feast of a great many oxen,
> fatlings, and sheep, and he has invited all the king's son and Abiathar the
> priest, and Joab commander of the army; but he has not invited your servant
> Solomon. And so the eyes of all Israel are upon you, O lord king, to tell them
> who shall succeed my lord the king on the throne. Otherwise, when my lord the
> king lies down with his fathers, my son Solomon and I will be regarded as
> traitors'* (1 Kgs 1.17-21; JPS).

Fokkelman notes that the essential information is contained in
Nathan's version, which Bathsheba converts from his recommended
humble questions into a much stronger, assertive declaration.[37] With
her direct remark, 'You know nothing about' Adonijah's making himself king, Bathsheba 'dares to confront David squarely with his impotence'.[38] These are not the words of a submissive, docile woman.
Either Bathsheba has undergone a complete change of personality
since David seduced her or she then, as now, is as much in control of

---

37.   Fokkelman: 'She begins by making David feel guilty, 17b-d: you have forgotten your promise and slighted your son Solomon. The reproach which follows,
implying incompetence as father and king and cached in the words of v. 18, evokes
a sense of failure. In 19b David will feel let down if not betrayed. Everyone, to his
exclusion, is busy arranging the succession. His own sons are agitating behind his
back and even his staunch friend Abiathar has deserted him. The name Joab is
useful in hinting at great rancour; he is the man with more political know-how that
David (II Sam 19.19). It is very contriving of Bathsheba to use this against Adonijah
and in Solomon's favour. In v. 19c she plays on David's sympathy: Solomon is
loyal to you but see how isolated he is. She continues in similar fashion in v. 21.
The latter period activates a mixture of compassion (my wife and child, their last
hour has struck!) and guilt feelings (how could he be so cruel as not to come to
their aid). As compensation, Bathsheba puts David back on the pedestal of
absolute power in v. 20 and her underlying message is one of consolation: nothing
is lost yet, if you would only act quickly. Although Bathsheba probably says
nothing which is factually incorrect, her address at the same time consists of total
and refined manipulation' (*Narrative Art*, pp. 357-58).
38.   Fokkelman, *Narrative Art*, p. 356.

her fate as she could be in a patriarchal society. Her setting David up for seduction, according to this reading, is no more shocking than her using Yahweh's name to 'reinforce' a vow that most likely had not taken place—but is validated by a *subsequent* vow. Bathsheba is revealed as a resourceful, determined woman who struggles within the system—with any means at hand—to achieve her goals.

As pre-arranged, Nathan enters and corroborates Bathsheba's words, using phrases closer to those of Bathsheba than the ones he had originally proposed for her.

Nathan's new version:

> O lord king, you must have said, 'Adonijah shall succeed me as king, and he shall sit upon my throne'. For he has gone down today, and *has prepared a sacrificial feast of a great many oxen, fatlings, and sheep. He invited all the king's sons* and the army officers *and Abiathar the priest*. At this very moment they are eating and drinking with him, and they are shouting, 'Long live King Adonijah!' But he did not invite me, your servant, or the priest Zadok, or Benaiah the son of Jehoida, or *your servant Solomon*. Can this decision have come from my lord the king, without your telling your servant *who is to succeed to the throne of my lord the king*? (1 Kgs 1.23-27; JPS).

The implication is that Nathan has listened, and his adoption of Bathsheba's words recognizes not only the merit of Bathsheba's presentation but also the force of her personality. We must keep in mind that this is a high-ranking male prophet using—following—the words of a woman. Nathan and Bathsheba are cooperating, using or leaving out each other's words, adding their own touches, to their mutual advantage.

The scene ends with David calling Bathsheba back into his presence. This time, Bathsheba does not bow upon her entrance; she stands and awaits David's response to her appeal and Nathan's. David then swears an oath, using the very words Bathsheba had used to describe his earlier oath (v. 13de = v. 17cd), claimed by Bathsheba and Nathan, as the core of the new and validating vow. Bathsheba's evocation of 'by Yahweh *your* God' (1 Kgs 1.17)—which hedges her involvement with the alleged earlier oath—is changed to a larger perspective by David: 'I have sworn by Yahweh, the God of Israel' (1.30).

With David's oath to make Solomon his successor 'this very day' (v. 30), Bathsheba does prostrate herself before him, 'with her face to the ground, does obeisance to the king, and says, "May my lord King David live for ever!"' (v. 31). David, she implies, will live on in her son Solomon. Bathsheba and Nathan have accomplished their goal: Solomon becomes king, Nathan remains a court prophet and Bathsheba remains in a position of power, shifting from king's wife to king's mother.

Bathsheba, King's Mother

No sooner is David buried than Adonijah comes to ask Bathsheba, now mother of the king, to act as intermediary to Solomon in Adonijah's desire to have Abishag the Shunammite—formerly ministering to David—as wife. Bathsheba is initially cautious, asking, 'Do you come peaceably?' (1 Kgs 2.13). Assuring her that he does come peaceably, Adonijah shows Bathsheba the respect due the king's mother by asking permission to speak: 'I have something to say to you' (v. 14), and she grants him that permission. Adonijah initially acknowledges the political situation: the kingship was his and has 'become his brother's, for it was his from the Lord' (v. 15), thus accepting the loss of kingship. However, he still has one request to make of Bathsheba, and she once more grants him permission to speak. Observing the close relationship between mother-queen and son-king, Adonijah believes 'he (Solomon) will not refuse you' (v. 17). Adonijah desires that Bathsheba act as negotiator between himself and Solomon to get Abishag the Shunammite as wife.

This sequence demonstrates the deference and honor accorded the king's mother both from the court and from her son ('he will not refuse you'). King Solomon does honor his mother's appearance, rising to meet her and bowing down to her, sitting on his throne but commanding a seat be brought 'for the king's mother; and she sat on his right' (v. 19). Bathsheba asks for 'one small request', and 'do not refuse me' (v. 20). Solomon graciously acquiesces, 'Make your request, my mother; for I will not refuse you' (v. 20). However, when Bathsheba asks that Abishag the Shunammite be given his brother Adonijah as wife, King Solomon immediately repudiates his promise to his mother:

> And why do you ask Abishag the Shunammite for Adonijah? Ask for him the kingdom also; for he is my elder brother, and on his side are Abiathar the priest and Joab the son of Zeruiah. Then King Solomon swore by the Lord, saying, 'God do so to me and more also if this word does not cost Adonijah his life! Now therefore as the Lord lives, who has established me, and who has made me a house, as he promised, Adonijah shall be put to death this day' (1 Kgs. 2.22-24; JPS).

Although the text says that David never 'knew' her, Abishag does belong to the king's concubines, and is therefore symbolic of the king's sexual/political power. Whoever sleeps with the king's women is, implicitly, king; for example, in the political intrigue over David's heir to the throne, Solomon's brother Absalom challenged David's kingship by sleeping with David's concubines. He took this action on the advice of Ahitophel, whose counsel was esteemed and surely reflected the custom of the people (2 Sam. 16.20-23). In this context, where sexual prowess is clearly equated with political prowess, this is a precarious move by Adonijah. Significantly, in his appeal to Bathsheba, Adonijah minimizes his claim to political power by *asking* Solomon for Abishag, instead of taking her. He does not threaten Solomon, though the throne is his by right of primogeniture. But Bathsheba does not convey these mitigating aspects to Solomon. It is difficult to imagine this resourceful woman to be so dull with regard to court etiquette and intrigues that she presents Adonijah's case naively. I suggest that, although she asks Solomon not to refuse her, her presentation of Adonijah's case assures that Solomon *will refuse*, thus eliminating a potential rival for the throne and a potential danger to her and her son's position.

Bathsheba completes the paradigm established by Ruth and Tamar, and she develops that paradigm in a way impossible to the earlier ancestresses of kings. Reading Bathsheba in this light renders her wholly consistent in the two phases of her life recorded in the text: as conceiving woman and as protecting/guiding mother. Motherhood—conception and its continuation as nurturing/protecting—is presented as the dominating force for a woman. Sexual drive is ascribed to males: David desires Bathsheba and takes her, but sexual drive is denied esteemed future mothers of patriarchs and kings in the Davidic line.

Bathsheba's deceptive 'appeal' to Solomon is her last appearance. There is no mention of her death in the text. Once she has contributed to Solomon's being securely established on the throne (1 Kgs 2), her mothering role seems to be complete—and she is secure in her position as king's mother. Similarly, Tamar and Ruth disappear from the text when their roles as mother have been fulfilled. The ancestresses were resourceful bearers of sons in the royal lineage, but their stories relate no further roles in their sons' lives. In this reading, Bathsheba—like her predecessors—takes an enterprising role in conception and continues to take a dynamic role in her son's struggle for power. She extends the protecting and guiding of motherhood into her son's manhood; but when the possibility of mothering no longer exists—when her son is secure in the kingship—she too disappears from the text.

Bathsheba is neither temptress nor victim—and she is both. Her

TAMAR AND THE 'COAT OF MANY COLORS'

Adrien Janis Bledstein

The 'coat of many colors', worn by Joseph in Hebrew Scriptures, is possibly the most famous garment in the Western world. However, readers of the King James Version of the Bible may not realize that one other person in the Bible, Tamar the daughter of King David, also wore the k^etonet passîm (כתנת פסים), mostly translated 'a garment of divers colors' (2 Sam. 13.18-19).

You will remember that Jacob sent his favorite son on a journey to report on the well-being of his half-brothers and the herds. From a distance, his brothers recognized Joseph in the garment that announced his favored status in the family. Conspiring to kill this 'master of dreams', they instead stripped him of his 'coat of many colors', threw him in a pit, then sold him as a slave (Gen. 37.12-28).

Also commissioned by her father, Princess Tamar went to the house of her half-brother Amnon, who claimed to be ill. Wearing the k^etonet passîm, she shaped and baked dough in his sight, poured something and brought the food to an inner chamber, to his bedside, so that he might eat. He grabbed hold of her, raped her, then threw her out (2 Sam. 13.6-18).

Is it not remarkable that each person appareled in the k^etonet passîm was authorized by his or her father to perform a service and, during the performance, each was abused by brothers then cast out?

In a tantalizing version of the Joseph episode, *Targum Pseudo-Jonathan* translated Joseph's garment as pargôd (פרגוד), from a Greek word of Semitic origin meaning 'separation', 'curtain' or 'veil'.[1] In the Bible, before Joseph found his brothers, he encountered a stranger. According to this targum, the stranger said, 'I heard *from behind the curtain* (pargôdā, פרגודא) that your brothers are in Dothan' (Gen. 37.17). Through the addition of 'from behind the curtain' to the biblical verse and the word choice for Joseph's garment, Jonathan linked the 'coat of

---

1. J. Bowker, *The Targums and Rabbinic Literature: An Introduction to Jewish Interpretations of Scripture* (London: Cambridge University Press, 1969), p. 237.

many colors' to the heavenly curtain from behind which the divine
speaks to divine messengers and humans in post-biblical Jewish mid-
rash. This essay on Tamar's 'coat of divers colors' explores the meaning of this costume in the biblical world and surrounding cultures. I
suggest that Jonathan's linking of the garment with receiving divine
words has ancient roots.

What, then, would the meaning of the costume imply regarding
each narrative, especially for Tamar? Post-biblical interpretations of
the *k^{e}tonet passîm* invite speculation.

Post-Biblical Translations

Joseph's (and Tamar's) 'technicolor dream coat' may not be distinctive
because of its coloring: the *k^{e}tonet* indicates a garment of some sort,
but *passîm* does not mean color. The striped robe popular in children's
illustrated Bibles may have arisen from the modern Hebrew meaning
of *pas* as 'strip' or 'stripe', or from an Aramaic translation in *Targum
Onqelos*.[2] Because *pas* in biblical Hebrew means 'extremity', 'border'
and 'vanishing', rabbinic commentators conjured a garment 'so light
and delicate that it could be crushed and concealed in the closed palm
of one hand'.[3] For others, *pas* as 'extremity' indicated the sole of the
foot or palm of the hand, giving rise to various translations such as 'a
long robe with sleeves' (NRSV), 'an ankle-length garment', 'a long-
sleeved robe'; or, in combination, 'a long-sleeved tunic reaching to the
ankle'.[4]

Adopting 'long robe with sleeves' as the preferred translation, in

---

2.   B. Grossfeld, *The Targum Onqelos to Genesis: Translated with a Critical Introduction, Apparatus, and Notes* (Wilmington, DE: Michael Glazier, 1988), p. 126.

3.   L. Ginzburg, *Legends of the Jews* (7 vols.; Philadelphia: Jewish Publication
Society, 1909), II, p. 7.

4.   For 'ankle-length', see also the Oxford Bible. C. Westermann surmises: 'It
is a special garment, a sleeved tunic (not a "coat of many colors"), according to
2 Samuel 13.18 the costume of a princess, an ankle-length tunic...that designates
high rank. This gift to Joseph is the first occurrence of the clothing motif, which
will turn up repeatedly throughout the narrative. The author presupposes the
great social significance of clothing, for millennia one of the most striking evi-
dences of social stratification. It is this tunic, not Joseph's dreams, that first poses
the question: May a brother be thus exalted above his other brothers?' (*Genesis*
[Grand Rapids, MI: Eerdmans, 1987], pp. 262-63). Because the garment was worn
by both a man and a woman, the rabbis imagined: 'Joseph had grown very vain,
daubed his eyes with kohl, dressed his locks like a woman, walked mincingly, and
wore a long-sleeved tunic which Jacob had given him' (*Gen. R.* 84; R. Graves and
R. Patai, *Hebrew Myths* [New York: Greenwich House, 1983], p. 250).

1959 Israeli archaeologists pointed to a fifteenth-century BCE Egyptian tomb painting found at Thebes. Several wealthy, tribute-bearing Canaanites wore long-sleeved fitted garments

> made of pieces of cloth stitched together with embroidery that emphasized the lines of the garment. The sleeves were unusually long, reaching to the elbow and sometimes even as far as the wrists. Usually a scarf of the same cloth was worn with the coat, being wound in a spiral round the waist. Sometimes the cloth was of a different colour inside and out and therefore had a multi-coloured appearance when worn in folds and wound round the body: the lower edge of the garment was hemmed.[5]

However, this garment is depicted on many men and no women. Three years later, editors of *The Interpreter's Dictionary of the Bible* looked for garments worn by both men and women and pointed to a nineteenth-century BCE extended mural on a wall of the tomb of an Egyptian noble at Beni-hasan. Asiatics appear in sleeveless tunics reaching to the knee or midway down the calf, and attached at one shoulder. Reflecting the post-biblical meaning of *pas* as 'strip' or 'stripe', colorful geometric designs decorate lengthwise stripes.[6] As the garment is worn by several men and women, one may wonder if this common garment would incite murderous hatred in Joseph's brothers.

In 1964, E.A. Speiser took another tack and bluntly asserted: 'The traditional "coat of many colors", and the variant "coat with sleeves" are sheer guesses from the context; nor is there anything remarkable about either colors or sleeves'.[7] Drawing upon A. Leo Oppenheim's suggestion, Speiser wondered if the garment was distinguished as an

---

5. B. Mazar (ed.), *Views of the Biblical World* (4 vols.; Jerusalem: International Publishing Company, 1959), I, p. 94. Also *ANEP*, p. 47; *The Illustrated Bible Dictionary* (Leicester: Inter-Varsity Press, 1980), I, p. 396; Tomb 63 at the British Museum, no. 37991.

6. Editors of the *Interpreter's Dictionary of the Bible* also offered from written records 'the colorful garment decorated with *birmu*, which is a narrow band woven from wool threads of assorted colors' worn by both Pharaoh Necho and women. 'These narrow, bright strips are described in the Annals of Ashurnasirpal II [883-859 BCE] as the garb of two hundred females' (*IDB*, II, p. 983). Also, *Tyndale's Illustrated Bible Dictionary* (Leicester: Inter-Varsity Press, 1980), II, p. 813, 'Joseph' (at Beni Hasan, on the wall of the tomb of Khnum-hotep III).

7. E.A. Speiser, *Genesis* (AB, 1; Garden City, NY: Doubleday, 1964), p. 289; also Radak (David Kimchi, 1160–1235 CE, a rabbinic commentator); JPSV; AV; LXX and V.; and S.R. Driver, *Notes on the Hebrew Text and the Topography of the Books of Samuel* (Oxford: Clarendon Press, 1960), pp. 299-300

'ornamented tunic' (adopted by the NJPSV), like a ceremonial robe listed as draped about the statue of a goddess during the time of Nebuchadnezzar II (605–562 BCE).[8] The description resembles an embroidered divine and royal garment which became fashionable in Assyria during the ninth through seventh centuries BCE. Twentieth-century discoveries of other Aramaic translations support this interpretation, with an 'embroidered ornamented garment'.[9] Though Speiser and Oppenheim connect the ornamented garment of the goddess Nana with Joseph's, they do not spell out the implications for the biblical texts in which Joseph and Tamar wear the apparel of a goddess. Furthermore, Speiser dates the composition of the Joseph narrative to the tenth century BCE, when Tamar the daughter of David lived, three hundred years before Nebuchadnezzar. The search goes on.

Drawing on Greek, Latin, Syriac and Arabic cognates, folklorist T. Gaster (1969) speculated 'coat of lengths', 'a quilted or patchwork tunic', though he preferred imagining an ankle-length, priestly robe.[10]

---

8.   Both the New Jewish Publication Society translation and E. Fox's *In the Beginning: A New Rendition of the Book of Genesis* (New York: Schocken Books, 1983) 'ornamented coat' are subsequent to Speiser's discussion: 'Cuneiform inventories may shed light on the garment in question. Among various types of clothing listed in the texts, there is one called *kitu* (or *kutinnu*) *pisannu* (cf. A.L. Oppenheim, 'The Golden Garments of the Gods', *JNES* 8 [1949], p. 177). The important thing there, besides the close external correspondence with the Heb. phrase, is that the article so described was a ceremonial robe which could be draped about statues of goddesses, and had various gold ornaments sewed on it. Some of these ornaments would occasionally come undone and need to be sent to the proper craftsmen for repairs, hence the notation in the inventories. If the comparison is valid—and there are several things in its favor—the second element in the Heb. phrase, i.e., *passim*, would be an adaptation of Akk. *pisannu*, a technical term denoting appliqué ornaments on costly vests and bodices' (p. 290). The garment in question is put in the Joseph tale by a narrator Speiser places in the tenth century BCE, possibly a contemporary of the Court Narrator of 2 Samuel 13 (Speiser, *Genesis*, p. xxviii). In 'The Golden Garments of the Gods', the *JNES* article cited above by Speiser, A. Leo Oppenheim dates the garment of the goddess to the Neo-Babylonian period, specifically to the 19th and 32nd years of Nebuchadnezzar II (pp. 177 and 179).

9.   M. McNamara, *Targum Neofiti 1: Genesis: Translated, with Apparatus and Notes* (Collegeville, MN: Liturgical Press, 1992), p. 171.

10.   T.H. Gaster elaborated: 'Now *pasim* (sic) is the plural of the word *pas*, which normally means "lengths, extension". Literally, therefore, the garment was a "coat of lengths". [8: "the word occurs in this sense in post-Biblical Hebrew and in Syriac. Cognate are Arabic *f-sh-y*, 'extend' and Heb. *p-s-h*. In Ps. 72.16 the expression *pissat bar* means simply 'an expanse (RSV: abundance) of corn', and no emen-

The idea of a 'patchwork tunic' resembles a suggestion by Nahum Sarna two decades later. He drew attention to an eighteenth-century BCE mural 'in the palace of King Zimri-lim at Mari, in southeast Syria, [which] shows figures dressed in garments made of many small rectangles of multicolored cloth'.[11] The dress he points to occurs frequently in Mesopotamia on steles, plaques, statues, wall reliefs, paintings, amulets and hundreds of cylinder seals from c. 2400 to 1400 BCE, encompassing the lifetime of Joseph.

These ankle-length, flounced garments with stripes or strips which are thick or thin, straight or wavy, are represented with five to as many as twelve tiers of either pleated fabric or strips of woven or felted wool. Archaized versions of both flouncing and the divine horned headdress appear as late as 740 BCE. Sarna makes no mention of the status of those who wore flounced garments and what that might mean in the biblical texts.

With all these imaginative proposals, one may safely assume that so far there is no consensus regarding the meaning of *k^{e}tonet passîm*. What we know is that both a favorite son of a chief and a virgin daughter of a king wore the *k^{e}tonet passîm*. Each of them was commissioned by his or her father: the man as a deputy to oversee his brothers and his father's possessions; the woman to attend an ailing member of the royal family. Other clues emerge as we examine biblical texts.

dation is needed".] The Greek Septuagint and some of the other ancient translators took this to mean a garment made out of various lengths of different materials— that is, a kind of quilted or patchwork tunic, [9: LXX *poikilos chiton*; Vulg.: tunica polymita; similarly the Syriac Peshitta at II Sam. 13.18-19.], and it is from this interpretation that the familiar "coat of many colors" is derived'. T.H. Gaster, *Myth, Legend, and Custom in the Old Testament* (New York: Harper & Row, 1969), pp. 216 and 37. Gaster's connection of Hebrew פס with Arabic *psy* is questioned by Cyrus Gordon in correspondence.

11.   N. Sarna, *Genesis* (Jewish Publication Society Torah Commentary; Philadelphia/Jerusalem: The Jewish Publication Society, 1989), p. 255. The wall paintings from Zimri-lim's palace are on display at the Louvre. The colors represented are those natural to sheep: 'Sheep's wool ranges in color from black and dark brown, through the reddish and buff or grey colors typical of wild sheep, to white'. E.J.W. Barber, *Prehistoric Textiles* (Princeton: Princeton University Press, 1991), p. 21. The occasional pale blue strip may be dyed white wool.

Figure 1. *Priest and Minor Goddess Wearing Flounced Garments, from a mural at the palace of Zimri-lim, Mari, 17th century* BCE.

Textual Clues

In the Bible, a *kᵉtonet* is a garment which appears 29 times, of which 20 indicate a protective, sacred tunic worn by priests. 'The holy linen coat' (Lev. 16.4) was worn by Aaron, the high priest, when he went within the holy of holies of the tabernacle to burn incense before the Ark of the Covenant. *kᵉtonet* here served as an undergarment and was part of the 'holy clothing' (Exod. 28.4) which included the breast-plate, ephod, robe (*meʿîl*) and 'broidered' (AV), 'chequered' (NEB), or 'fringed' (NJPSV) tunic (*kᵉtonet tašbēs*).[12] It is the garment made for Aaron and his four sons, the priests (Exod. 28.39, 40; 29.5; 39.27; 40.14).

There are notable exceptions to the priestly garment. For Adam and Eve, YHWH made 'coats of skins' (Gen. 3.21) to shield them as they were sent away from the Garden of Eden. Three high officials wear a *ktnt*, an emblem of high office: Hushai (King David's 'friend', 2 Sam. 15.32, 37),[13] Shebna and Eliakim, two who were doomed to destruc-

12. The 'broidered' or 'checkered' garment may be reminiscent of a flounced garment of strips. Elsewhere this term is 'weave in chequer or plaited work' (BDB, p. 990). See the following discussion of the history of the flounced garment.

13. 'Friend of the king' is an official title held also by Solomon's officer, Zabud, son of Nathan 'priest' (1 Kgs 4.5). He could be a son of Nathan the prophet or Solomon's brother, another son of Bathsheba (1 Chron. 3.5). Neither is identified as Levitical or a descendant of Aaron. This seems to be another example of a royal,

tion in Isaiah (22.15-25). Isaiah predicted that Eliakim would become 'father to the inhabitants of Jerusalem and to the house of Judah' (Isa. 22.21), just as Joseph was a 'father to Pharaoh' in Egypt (Gen. 45.8). However, the predicted rise of Eliakim to high office is part of a build-up curse. This kind of curse first paints a detailed, glowing picture of greatness or good fortune. The punch line turns everything upside down in one devastating statement. Through this curse, Isaiah makes clear that neither Shebna nor Eliakim will be protected by the special garment.

As one who regularly made sacrifices, Job wore a priestly garment, called מְעִלוֹ, *me'ilô* in Job 1.20. Later he referred to his garment as a *ketonet* (30.18). The woman in the Song of Songs (5.3) has removed her *ketonet* in preparation for retiring for the night. She is the only woman aside from Tamar, daughter of King David, who wears a *ketonet*, so the connotation may be intended to imply royal status. Whether or not the 'Cultic Theory' or 'sacred marriage' mode of interpretation is correct about elements in the cultural background of the development of the Song, *ketonet* here may indicate that the woman playfully portrays herself wearing a sacred garment as a priestess-bride, and that her lover is a god. A Sumerian 'sacred marriage' song is suggestive. In response to her lover's complaint that she shut herself in her house, the goddess sings that she washed and dressed herself 'in the garments of queenship, of the queenship of heaven'.[14]

It is remarkable that six of the nine non-priests and two of Aaron's four sons who wore a *ketonet* suffered disaster. As we have seen, Adam and Eve were unique in that YHWH gave them *ketonet* of skins to protect them outside of Eden. Tamar, Joseph, Job, the woman in the Song of Songs, Shebna and Eliakim were not so blessed. For them, the *ketonet* served to symbolize a high status lost. The only non-priest who wore the *ketonet* and remained relatively unscathed was Hushai, David's friend. From this review we see that, for the majority who wore the *ketonet*, there was an element of danger. Wearing a *ketonet* appears to indicate aristocratic but, most often, sacred status. The *ketonet passîm*, it seems to me, was a special form of this high-status, sacred garb.

Another term provides information concerning the garment Tamar wore. After Amnon raped her and commanded his servant: 'Put this

non-Levitical priesthood indicated in 2 Sam. 8.18 and separate from those responsible for the Ark.

14. M. Pope, *Song of Songs* (AB, 7C; Garden City, NY: Doubleday, 1977), p. 515; see also pp. 42-44 and 514-17.

out from me and bolt the door after her', we read: 'Now she had a *kᵉtonet passîm* on her; for with such robes (*meʿîlîm*, מְעִ[י]לִים) were the king's daughters that were virgins apparelled' (2 Sam. 13.18-19, JPSV). In English translation, that virgin princesses wore some sort of distinguishing robe seems straightforward. However, the kind of robe Tamar wore has made translators uncomfortable. The NRSV emends the Hebrew *meʿîlîm* to *mēʿōlām* (מעולם), 'from of old', so translates: 'for this is how the virgin daughters of the king were clothed *in earlier times*'. P. Kyle McCarter prefers a different emendation, *mēʿᵃlûmîm* (מעלומים), 'from puberty on'.[15] Other commentators read the statement as a gloss, and translations often enclose the remark in parentheses. For example, NRSV:

> He called the young man who served him and said, 'Put this woman out of my presence, and bolt the door after her'. (Now she was wearing a long robe with sleeves; for this is how the virgin daughters of the king were clothed in earlier times.) So his servant put her out, and bolted the door after her (2 Sam. 13.18-19).

Though *meʿîl* in modern Hebrew is an outer garment as common as a scarf or a shoe, the apparent need of translators to emend the word prompted me to inquire: who wore a *meʿîl* in the Bible? Except for Tamar, *meʿîlîm* were worn only by men, primarily priests. One was the priest-prophet-leader of the people Samuel. His mother, before he was physically conceived, devoted him to serve YHWH and yearly made him the garment (*meʿîl*) to wear in his service at the sanctuary (1 Sam. 2.19). Later Samuel wore a *meʿîl* in his official capacity as prophet-priest (1 Sam. 15.27). King Saul wore a *meʿîl* to battle (1 Sam. 24.5, 12). This was part of Jonathan's princely attire which he conferred on David after Goliath was slain (1 Sam. 18.4). In a procession with the Ark of the Covenant King David, the Levites and singers all wore the sacred robe (*meʿîl*, 1 Chron. 15.27).[16] It may have been a divine garment as well. The ghost of Samuel, raised by the woman of Endor in 1 Samuel 28, appeared as an *ʾelōhîm*, a divine being who was in the form of 'an old man enveloped with *meʿîl*' (1 Sam. 28.13-14), the

15. P.K. McCarter, *Samuel* (2 vols.; AB; Garden City, NY: Doubleday, 1984), II, pp. 315 and 318-19.
16. According to 1 Chron. 25.5-6, some women may have been singers in the House of the Lord. The daughters of 'Heman, the seer of the king' are mentioned, though not named, along with his sons: 'all these were under the charge of their father for the singing in the House of the Lord, to the accompaniment of cymbals, harps and lyres' (1 Chron. 25.6).

sacred garment he wore when alive. In Exodus and Leviticus, the high priest Aaron and his four sons wore *me'îlîm*.[17]

In each instance, the garment indicates sacred and/or royal attire. The use of *me'îl* in these contexts, combined with Tamar's performing a healing or purification ritual,[18] leads me to surmise that we are meant to understand that Tamar's *k^etonet passîm*, identified as a *me'îl*, served to confirm that she was a royal priestess. In support of this possibility 2 Sam. 8.18 may be read, 'and David's children were priests (כהנים)', indicating there was at the time a royal priesthood, which might have included daughters, and was separate from the male priesthood responsible for the Ark of the Covenant.

If we acknowledge that Tamar could have been a royal priestess, then the insertion regarding her apparel becomes an emphatic statement rather than a parenthetic gloss:

> Though she had on her *k^etonet passîm*, for such priestly robes (*me'îlîm*) will virgin daughters of the king wear, nonetheless, his servant brought her out and bolted the door after her. So Tamar put ashes on her head, tore the *k^etonet passîm* that was on her, put her hand on her head, and went her way crying aloud.[19]

The reader is reminded at this dramatic juncture that Tamar was commissioned by her father the king to attend to her ailing brother, the first-born son of David. The identification of *k^etonet passîm* as a *me'îl* strongly suggests that Tamar was a royal priestess whose duties included some sort of divine inquiry/ritual purification for ill members of the royal house.[20] In a Hittite text by a woman healer, feeding

---

17. Priests: Exod. 28.4, 31, 14; 29.5, 39; Lev. 8.7. M. Jastrow notes that the robe was especially worn by the high priest (*Dictionary of the Talmud Babli, Yerushalmi, Midrashic Literature and Targumim* [2 vols.; New York: Pardes Publishing House, 1943], II, p. 815).

18. A. Bledstein, 'Was *Habbiyâ* a Healing Ritual Performed by a Woman in King David's House?', *BR* 38 (1992), pp. 15-31. From my current research, I have come to suspect that she was performing a purification ritual called, perhaps, 'purity of Ya', *bôr-Yāh*.

19. For variety in translating the conjunction ו as 'notwithstanding' and 'so', see BDB, pp. 252-53

20. 'Religion plays an important part in the history of costume. Early in human history the man [sic] of insight must have been set apart from his fellows as definitely as was the man of brawn. In the hands of such a man certain objects seemed to be endowed with supernatural power to cure the sick and expel evil. Symbols of these fearful and beneficent agents were adopted, the one to appease, the other to revere, and there we have the beginning of religious vestments and ritual' (B. Payne, *The History of Costume: From the Ancient Egyptians to the Twentieth Century* [New York: Harper and Row, 1965], p. 4.)

the sacrificer in his home at his bedside—as Tamar was about to do with Amnon—was meant to induce a dream which would be interpreted by the woman performing the rite. It is possible that Tamar was considered a 'mistress of dreams', as Joseph was indeed a 'master of dreams', though contemptuously called so by his brothers (Gen. 37.19).

When I began the search for the *k^etonet passîm*, the emendation 'from of old' made me wonder if 'virgin daughters of the king' in the context of performing a ritual for a member of the royal house might be a title, a designation with a history. What I found convinced me that no emendation of *me'îlîm* is necessary once we recognize that Tamar was a royal priestess. This is borne out when we examine the history of 'virgin daughters of the king', who wore (during the period Joseph lived, 17th century BCE) what I believe was meant by the *k^etonet passîm*: the tiered garment of white, gray, beige, brown and black strips worn, for one example, by 'minor goddesses' and the priest painted on the palace walls at Mari, alluded to by Sarna. The status and function of humans who were depicted in ancient art wearing this particular fashion will, I believe, explain why Joseph, the 'master of dreams' (בעל החלמות, Gen. 37.19) who later in Egypt excelled at management, as a youth wore the same type of distinguishing garment worn by Tamar, a priestess-princess during King David's reign.

'Virgin Daughters of the King'

In Mesopotamia, archaeologists have unearthed information about sixteen kings' daughters who were appointed by their royal fathers or brothers as high priestesses. These women believed they were wedded to the god of the city temple. Though there are gaps in the archaeological evidence, records of these royal priestesses span eighteen centuries, from c. 2400 to 540 BCE, encompassing the lifetimes of both Joseph and Tamar.[21] One of the earliest of these priestesses was Enheduanna, daughter of Sargon of Akkad (c. 2350 BCE).

In establishing his dynasty, Sargon secured Ur through the religious-political installation of Enheduanna as the high priestess at Ur (Abraham's homeland, Gen. 11.27-31) to serve at the temple which was dedicated to Nanna, the moon god, and his spouse Ningal. This royal priestess authored hymns which, according to W.W. Hallo, were

---

21. For a list of royal high priestesses see P.N. Weadock, 'The *Giparu* at Ur', *Iraq* 37 (1975), pp. 127-28.

religiously and politically innovative and set a literary standard for centuries.[22] On an inscribed fragmentary calcite disc, Enheduanna is depicted performing a ritual and wears an ankle-length version of the flounced garment portrayed later at Mari. A cape of two flounces covers both shoulders and arms.[23] Except for a period of exile during political disruption, she functioned as high priestess at Ur into the reign of her nephew, priest-king Naram-Sin (c. 2300 BCE), portrayed on a stele wearing a version of the flounced garment which leaves one shoulder bare.[24]

Thus we see that both a royal priestess and a king-priest wore the flounced garment. This garb was preceded in earliest depictions by garments made of sheep and goat skins worn by commoners, leaders and deities. Mesopotamian artistic representations of these animal skins make it appear that the fleece or hair was in tiers, the one above overlapping the one below, resembling what we call flouncing. This is very likely what the narrator had in mind for the k*e*tonet of skins YHWH made for Adam and Eve in Gen. 3.21.

Wealth and high social status were indicated by increased length and by the number of rows in what later appear to be manufactured flounces, probably loosely looped tufts attached to a woven backing as in carpet making.[25] As skins with fleece or hair gave way to man-ufactured wool garments, the aristocracy and deities continued to be portrayed in ankle-length, flounced garments with stripes, straight or wavy, instead of rows of tufts. The rows of tufts seem to me a tran-sition from skins to the flounced garment of woven strips, worn by the high priestess and priest-king in 2300 BCE.

Apparently the flounced garment was gathered or pleated, as evi-denced in figures of gods with one foot on a mountain, so that the

22. W.W. Hallo, *The Exaltation of Inanna* (New Haven: Yale University Press, 1968), p. 1.

23. A photograph of the unreconstructed disc is found in C.L. Woolley, *Ur of the Chaldees* (revised by P. Moorey; Ithaca, NY: Cornell University Press, 1982), p. 127. The reconstructed disc, which obscures Enheduanna's conical headdress, is at the University of Pennsylvania Museum.

24. Hallo, *Exaltation*, p. 2. Elsewhere, Naram-Sin is portrayed as a warrior wearing 'the horned cap of divinity' by Tessa Rickards, illustrator in J. Black and A. Green, *Gods, Demons and Symbols of Ancient Mesopotamia: An Illustrated Dictionary* (London: British Museum Press, 1992), fig. 75. The stele of Naram-Sin is at the Istanbul Museum. See A. Parrot, *Sumer* (Paris: Gallimard, repr. 1980), p. 175, plate 211.

25. The length of the garment is used by scholars to determine the chronology of artifacts on which figures are depicted. S. Corbiau, 'Sumerian Dress Lengths as Chronological Data', *Iraq* 3 (1936), pp. 97-100.

spread of material becomes clear.[26] The expense in time and labor for the quantity of material of the finest quality woven wool required would limit the fashion in those days to be worn by only the highest class. Indeed, gradually the costume was reserved for representations of deities, and the fashion is much less in evidence after the fifteenth century BCE.

Due to disruptions in history and the fortuitous nature of archae-ology, a hiatus appears in the visual record. 'At the end of the 2nd and the beginning of the 1st millennium BCE we have another of the mysterious gaps in our knowledge which have occurred from time to time throughout the three-thousand-year history of the cylinder seal'.[27] Nonetheless, archaized representations of flounced garments appear from 1300 to as late as 700 BCE. Furthermore, cylinder seals with figures wearing the flounced garment appear far afield in both space and time, as seals were traded and reused for jewelry and amulets.[28] Recently unearthed, two inscribed Israelite seals from the latter half of the eighth century BCE depict high officials wearing flounced skirts—one short, one long.[29] Each seal reflects Egyptian artistic representation. However, the skirts and poses of each figure resemble the representation of a god from Ashur, in glazed brick from the same period.[30] The seals may depict the garment Isaiah had in mind when he declared against the arrogance of Shebna and Eliakim (Isa. 22.15-25).

By the fifteenth century BCE, the flounced garment of strips in Mes-opotamia clothes gods and goddesses, especially a figure art histori-ans call a 'minor goddess' or 'interceding goddess' who is seen lead-ing by the hand a worshiper, often a king or high official, toward a major deity. She holds her other hand up in supplication. Sometimes she is depicted standing behind the worshiper or between the

26. Parrot, *Sumer*, p. 193, fig. 237.

27. D. Collon, *First Impressions: Cylinder Seals in the Ancient Near East* (Chicago: University of Chicago Press; London: British Museum Publications, 1987), pp. 75 and 130.

28. A Babylonian seal was found at Platanos, Crete. See C.H. Gordon, *The Common Background of Greek and Hebrew Civilizations* (New York: W.W. Norton, 1965), p. 320. For distribution of seals in space and time see Donald M. Matthews, *Principles of Composition in Near Eastern Glyptic of the Later Second Millennium B.C.* (Göttingen: Vandenhoeck & Ruprecht, 1990), pp. 9-11.

29. A. Lemaire, 'Name of Israel's Last King Surfaces in a Private Collection', *BARev* 21.6 (1995), p. 51.

30. *ANEP*, #535; A. Parrot, *The Arts of Assyria* (New York: Golden Press, 1961), p. 71.

worshiper and the major god or goddess. This ubiquitous female figure in a flounced gown often wears a headdress with one set of horns, indicating that she is a minor goddess who serves to intercede between the mortal and the divine.

The Sumerian term for *entu*, the title of the high priestess, is NIN.DINGER, meaning 'lady (who is) a deity' or NIN-DINGIRA, 'lady/spouse of a god'.[31] From extant writings by two princess-priestesses, the previously mentioned Enheduanna and Enanedu daughter of Kudur-Mabuk and sister of Warad-Sin and Rim-Sin of Larsa (c. eighteenth century BCE), we hear that each prays for the life of the king.[32] Also, Naram-Sin's daughter, Enmenanna, successor to Enheduanna, characterized herself as 'spouse of Nanna [moon god], high priestess of Suen'.[33] The virginity of these women is suggested by Enanedu who describes herself as having 'loins suitable by (their) purity for the *entu*-ship'.[34] These texts indicate that the high priestess, considered the wife of a god, functioned as an intermediary between the royal house and the divine.

Furthermore, statues dedicated to goddesses look very much like seated priestesses wearing flounced garments. Their hands are folded in a gesture associated with receiving a revelation. In exile, Enheduanna complained: '(My) hands are no longer folded on the ritual couch, I may no longer reveal the pronouncements of Ningal to man'.[35] In another inscription, Enheduanna appears as 'the *entu* priestess, chosen for the pure "divine decrees" '.[36] Hallo discusses two functions of the high priestess. She performed lustration (purification rites) and was a dream interpreter. 'Ningal, like some other goddesses, was known as a patroness of dream interpretation, and the mention of the ritual couch (literally "fruitful, shining couch") suggests an incubation technique for eliciting the divine response.'[37]

Besides the above textual indications that priestesses conveyed divine words, a list of gods receiving offerings included two deceased *entu* priestesses as deities. The record of these offerings combined

31. *CAD* E 7' b, p. 173; Cyrus Gordon, correspondence.
32. Weadock, *'Giparu'*, p. 103. Benjamin Leftowitz wrote a valuable discussion of the duties and functions of high priestesses ('The En of Ur from Sargon of Akkad to Rim-Sin', unpublished manuscript, June 1, 1976).
33. Hallo, *Exaltation*, p. 11 n. 69.
34. Weadock, *'Giparu'*, p. 101.
35. Hallo, *Exaltation*, p. 31.
36. A. Sjøberg and E. Bergmann, 'The Collection of the Sumerian Temple Hymns', *TCS* (5 vols.; Locust Valley, NY: J.J. Augustin, 1969), III, p. 5 n. 1.
37. Hallo, *Exaltation*, pp. 57, 59, 60.

with written evidence that a living *entu* considered herself a wife of a god further confirm that these royal women were deified.[38]

Although most information about *entu* priestesses is from excavations at Ur, there is evidence of *giparus*, the sacred cloistered residence, of these priestesses, at other sites such as Haran (the homeland of matriarchs Rebekah, Leah and Rachel, mother of Joseph), indicating that royal priestesses served elsewhere as well.[39] The office of *entu*-ship is known at Ur from Sargon of Akkad to the Kassite period (c. 18th–12th centuries, 1730–1155 BCE) and to Nebuchadnezzar I (12th century, 1146–1123 BCE). It was thereafter re-instituted by Nabonidus (mid-6th century, 555–539 BCE), who reported having read inscriptions from Nebuchadnezzar and Sargon of Akkad.[40] Thus there is evidence of continuity over space and time, with variations on themes depending upon the peculiarities of each culture. For example at Emar, the woman chosen and installed in an elaborate ceremony was not a royal woman.[41]

However, in establishing a dynasty, the custom of a king appointing a daughter as a high priestess had a long history in the homeland of the royal ancestors of Judah-Israel. Conceivably, an Israelite version of the custom might have been instituted by David as he established his dynasty. This would explain the status and activity of Princess Tamar as an intermediary between an ill member of the royal family and YHWH.

Taking into consideration the history of virgin daughters of the king installed as high priestesses, I surmise that Tamar, a virgin daughter of King David, was a priestess sent by the king to perform a purification rite for her brother who was believed to be ill. She attended her brother attired in her sacred flounced garment, designated in Hebrew by *kᵉtonet passîm*, a special version of the priestly *meᶜîl*.

Tamar, Joseph and the 'Coat of Many Colors'

Until more explicit evidence is unearthed, I recommend that we imagine Tamar and Joseph wearing a version of the flounced garment which indicated high priesthood and was associated with the status of

---

38. Weadock, '*Giparu*', pp. 103-104.

39. R. Harris, '*Gipar*', in E. Ebeling *et al.* (eds.), *Reallexikon der Assyriologie und vorderasiatischen Archäologie* (8 vols.; Berlin: W. de Gruyter, 1968), III, p. 377.

40. Weadock, '*Giparu*', p. 112.

41. D. Fleming, *The Installation of Baal's High Priestess at Emar* (Atlanta, GA: Scholars Press, 1992), pp. 291-93.

a minor deity in Mesopotamia. Even if the reader favors a late date for the composition of both narratives, and adopts the Oppenheim/ Speiser suggestion of the 'ornamented tunic' which was draped about the image of a goddess in the sixth century BCE as the source and image for the *kᵉtonet passîm*, a puzzle common to both narratives remains: why would the biblical narratives emphasize that Joseph and Tamar each wore a divine garment? What does awareness of the cultural-historical-religious meaning of the flounced or the ornamented garment suggest for how we understand the biblical narratives?

With regard to Joseph, the *kᵉtonet passîm* which Jacob (roughly a contemporary of King Zimri-lim of Mari) made for his favorite, gifted son may have been intended to confer on him priesthood with the potential for sacred kingship—perhaps something on the order of Naram-Sin. Naram-Sin is depicted on two steles: in the one mentioned above, as high priest, he wears a flounced garment; in the other, the king is presented as a warrior with 'a horned helmet—a symbol of deification'.[42]

Joseph's gifts of dream interpretation and management, combined with his role as provider, correspond with the meaning of *en* in Sumerian. The office of an *enu* (masculine) or *entu* (feminine) included political as well as spiritual power. 'The word *en* in Sumerian has the basic meaning of successful economic manager; it implies the possession of a power to make things thrive, to produce abundance and prosperity, and from this power the authority to command the affairs of the community.'[43] Jacob recognized the potential of such gifts in Joseph and bestowed on him the garment signifying these gifts. Ironically, it was as second to Pharaoh in Egypt that Joseph, stripped of the flounced garment, performed as an *en* from Mesopotamia, the land of his birth.

By invoking the divine-royal Mesopotamian garment in the Joseph story, the narrator made clear to an ancient audience that YHWH, not Jacob, determined the circumstances under which Joseph would realize his gifts. Jacob was correct in assessing Joseph's gifts; however, the fond father's form of acknowledgment conveyed by the *kᵉtonet passîm* was a form of idolatry, by which he deified his son. Joseph, however, came to understand both his trauma in relation to his family and his exalted position in Egypt. Interpretation of dreams comes from God, he told Pharaoh (Gen. 41.16). 'It was not you', Joseph tells his

---

42. Y. Yadin, *The Art of Warfare in Biblical Lands in the Light of Archaeological Study* (2 vols.; New York: McGraw Hill, 1963), I, p. 150.

43. Weadock, '*Giparu*', p. 102.

brothers, 'but God who sent me here'—to save life (45.4-8). His words sound like appalling arrogance to a modern reader. However, to an ancient audience familiar with powerful men, such as Pharaoh and Naram-Sin, who literally believed they were gods, Joseph would appear humble as he acknowledges the divine and makes peace with his brothers.

With regard to Tamar, David's daughter, the description of her garment as that worn by virgin princess-priestesses occurs at the moment that Amnon orders his servant to throw her out. No longer a virgin with the pure loins suitable for *entu*-ship, she can no longer appear as a sanctified being and serve her deity wearing the *me'îl* as David had planned. The meaning of her attire is emphasized by the narrator to make vivid her tragedy as the servant, obeying his master, shoves her out and bolts the door.

This royal woman consecrated to serve YHWH and act as an intermediary for family members was not safe in the house of a brother. Her father David had behaved as if he were a divine being, like the legendary *b^enē 'elōhîm* who before the flood (Gen. 6.1-4) took any woman they chose. The king took a married woman, Bathsheba, and had her husband Uriah killed (2 Sam. 11). Tamar's trauma was presented in the context of David's punishment for setting himself above YHWH's law.

'So Tamar put ashes on her head, and tore the *k^etonet passîm* that was on her; put her hand on her head, and went her way crying aloud' (2 Sam. 13.19). Her gestures were associated with mourning, being stunned and devastated. She tore her distinguishing garment and publicly grieved in the streets of Jerusalem. Her brother Absalom hushed her: 'Keep silent, my sister, he is your brother, do not take this thing to heart' (2 Sam. 13.20), as if she should not take the event personally. Two years later Absalom avenged her humiliation by having Amnon killed, then went into exile to their grandfather, King Talmai of Geshur. No longer a public figure, Tamar remained 'desolated', 'appalled'[44] in her brother Absalom's house. What more can we know about Tamar?

The remarkable parallels in Joseph's and Tamar's experience with the *k^etonet passîm* lead me to *speculate*, from the history of the flounced garment and my sense of the biblical texts. Tamar was a 'mistress of dreams', that is why David sent her to the sick-bed of Amnon. She was literate, like Enheduanna and other kings' daughters whose

---

44. '*šōmēmâ*', BDB, p. 1030.

writings are extant. She understood both the political and personal implications of Amnon's desire and actions.

Let us notice what Tamar says in an effort to dissuade Amnon, when he (as Potiphar's wife coaxed Joseph, Gen. 39.7) said, 'Lie with me' (2 Sam. 13.11):

> No, my brother, do not force me; for no such thing ought to be done in Israel. Do not this sacrilege.[45] And I, where will I carry my shame? And you, you will be as one of the sacrilegious men in Israel. But now speak to the king, for he will not withhold me from you (2 Sam. 13.12-13).

We can imagine Tamar's words punctuated with physical struggle as Amnon uses his greater strength to overpower her. First, in his grip, she refuses his advance, emphasizing their relationship: 'No, my brother, do not force me'. Second, as he continues to hold her, she points out the larger context: rape is not acceptable in Israel, perhaps as opposed to other cultures. (Her words echo the Yahwist narrator's words regarding Dinah's rape in Gen. 34.7.) Third, she stresses the sacrilegious nature of his act. Fourth, she appeals to any shred of feeling he may have for her—'where will I carry my shame?' Fifth, she points out the social consequence for him. Sixth, she proposes marriage.

What does she mean by saying 'the king will not withhold me from you'? From Tamar's proposal under duress, a narrator in Genesis had Abraham claim that he and Sarah were half-sister and half-brother, with different fathers, in order to explain Abraham's lie (Gen. 20.2, 12). Perhaps Abraham's shrewd survival technique arose from Tamar's experience.[46]

Tamar's exalted position reflected on her full-brother Absalom. Amnon's infatuation, which turned to intense revulsion once he had his way with her, had political implications which Absalom immediately understood. When Absalom saw Tamar wailing with her *k*ᵉ*tonet passîm* torn, he did not ask what happened. He said, 'Has Amnon your brother been with you?' (2 Sam. 13.20), as if he had anticipated the possibility. Why?

The flounced garment of strips is the clue. David's appointment of Tamar to priesthood—like Jacob's singling out of Joseph—set the doubly royal siblings, Tamar and Absalom, above their half-brothers. Amnon, the oldest, had the most to lose. Like the gods and goddesses in other people's imaginations, Amnon's passion for Tamar in part

---

45. McCarter, *Samuel*, pp. 327-28.
46. A. Bledstein, 'The Trials of Sarah', *Judaism* 30.4 (1981), pp. 411-17.

had to do with appropriation of her spiritual-political power, signified by the *kᵉtonet passîm*. The narrator of the Court History of David was well aware of Egyptian, Canaanite and Mesopotamian myths of deities and their (to an Israelite Yahwist) outrageous sexual-political human behavior. Part of the power of these narratives arises from the narrator's appreciation of human vulnerability, and the underlying response of the writer to mythic tales and mythic imagination which informed the fantasies of people in that time.

When Tamar proposes marriage to Amnon, she is appealing to Amnon's fantasy. It is too late. His passion is violent, he wills not to hear her voice (לא אבה לשמע בקולה, 2 Sam. 13.14). After he has raped her and ordered her to leave, she addresses his sense of what is right in Israel. 'No, this great wrong to send me away is worse than what you did to me' (v. 16). Tamar either knew the law or set the precedent. An Israelite male who had sex with an unmarried woman was married to her, responsible for her well-being, and could not divorce her (Deut. 22.28-29). Again, Amnon 'willed not to hear her voice' (v. 16).

I cannot believe that this learned, gifted woman shriveled up and died in her brother Absalom's house. We are not told what happened to Tamar thereafter, as the Court History focuses on David and the demise of Absalom. I like to imagine that Tamar, like Joseph, came to understand her trauma and to use her gifts to benefit all Israel. The flounced garment distinguished her as a mistress of dreams. Her commission was to perform a ceremony to bring about healing. Bereft of the garment, she was free from the illusions woven into it by her father. Perhaps she wrote stories and poetry. I like to think that Tamar composed the core of the following prayer, recited even to this day by individual Jewish congregation members as the Priestly Blessing is chanted:

> Master of the World!
> I am Yours and my dreams are Yours.
> I have dreamed a dream and I do not know its meaning.
> May it be Your will, Adonoy, my God, and God of my ancestors,
> that all my dreams regarding myself,
> and regarding all of Israel be for the good;
> those I have dreamed concerning myself,
> and those I have dreamed about others,
> and those that others have dreamed about me.
> If they are good dreams, strengthen and reinforce them
> and may they be fulfilled in me and in them,
> like the dreams of Joseph [Gen. 37–50].
> But if they require curing, cure them like Miriam,
> the prophetess, from her *ṣāra'at* [Num. 12.1-15] and

like the waters of Marah through Moses, our teacher [Exod. 15.22-25].
As You transformed the curse of the wicked Balaam,
from a curse to a blessing [Num. 22.2–25.25],
so may You transform all my dreams
regarding myself and regarding all of Israel and all humankind for
goodness.
[May You] guard me,
[may You] be gracious to me
and [may You] accept me favorably, Amen.[47]

47. Adapted from A. Davis (ed. and trans.), *The Complete Metsudah Siddur: A New Linear Prayer Book* (New York: Metsudah Publications, 1990), pp. 815-22.

Part II

WOMEN AND MEN OF GOD IN THE BOOKS OF KINGS

CENTER OR FRINGE?
POSITIONING THE WIFE OF JEROBOAM (1 KINGS 14.1-18)*

Uta Schmidt

1. *Introduction*

'Center or fringe?'—'Fringe', most people might readily answer when questioned about the position of the wife of Jeroboam in the biblical story. Because most of them have never heard of her. And even if they had, they might have forgotten, because in some respects she really is a minor figure in 1 Kgs 14.1-18. However, a closer look at this story reveals that she is also at the center of the plot. Using a narratological approach, I will show that there cannot be an either-or decision, but that the wife of Jeroboam is both: at the center of the story and marginalized at the same time. Comparing her story to other women's stories in the books of Kings, one can see that in different ways they are also located in the tension between center and fringe.

2. *The Narratological Approach*

In order to analyze the structures of representation of women in narratives, I use a literary approach. In so doing, I rely heavily on the narratological approach of Mieke Bal.[1] Narratological analysis is especially useful in the search for structures, because it provides the tools to explore the actions of and relations among the actants of a narrative and therefore its structures and strategies of representation.

---

* Since 1997 I have been working on a PhD thesis about the structures of representation of women in the narratives of 1 and 2 Kings. This article originated from my work. It is based on a paper given to the 8th International Conference of the European Society of Women in Theological Research, in Hofgeismar, Germany, August 1999.

1. See M. Bal, *Narratology: Introduction to the Theory of Narrative* (Toronto: University of Toronto Press, 1985, repr. 1992); *idem*, 'Narrative Subjectivity', in *On Story-Telling: Essays in Narratology* (Sonoma, CA: Polebridge Press, 1991), pp. 146-70.

Narratological analysis enables one to determine, as closely as possible, the position of women—and also of men and of God—in the
structure of the narrative. It provides the means to explore how different perspectives of view and voice are employed in making the
narrative 'work'. A narratological model, with three different levels,
helps to make visible the interplay among the different aspects of a
story, and shows how a story produces as well as veils its various
meanings.[2]

One level is the structure of events, the plot, which is easy to find
by asking: What happens? Who acts? Who does not act? On this level
we look for the actions of the actants that constitute the events, and
for the relations among them. This is called the level of the 'fabula'.[3]
The next level of the narratological model is the level of the 'story'. It
is concerned with the way in which this structure of the narrative is
shown, by asking: How are the actants presented, turned into characters by their actions and their attributes? How is the information
concerning the places of action connected to create the impression of
space?[4] And then there is the level of the 'text'. This is concerned with
the text as the way in which the story is told, asking: Whose voice?
Who speaks? And in favor of whom?[5]

Looking at the story of the wife of Jeroboam I will concentrate on
some of its aspects: matters of identity and disguise, the issue of
'house as family unit' and 'house as place', and the question 'Where is
God?'. Thereby, I will show that the images of the woman constructed
on the different levels partly contradict each other and, in doing so,
generate a paradoxical structure of representation of women as
central as well as marginalized. With these aspects of analysis I plan
to open up different perspectives on the text, perspectives that do not

---

2. When using a literary approach to the text, a theoretical assumption
emerges: a text does not communicate the one and only meaning that its author
originally intended. Rather, the text is a texture, a communication in process
between the text, the author and the readers/hearers in their contexts. Therefore, a
text can always have more than one meaning. Cf. Elizabeth Struthers Malbon
and Janice Capel Anderson, 'Literary-Critical Methods', in E. Schüssler-Fiorenza
(ed.), *Searching the Scriptures. I. A Feminist Introduction* (London: SCM Press, 1994),
pp. 241-54; M.-T. Wacker, 'Geschichtliche, hermeneutische und methodologische
Grundlagen', in L. Schottroff, S. Schroer and M.-T. Wacker (eds.), *Feministische Exegese: Forschungserträge zur Bibel aus der Perspektive von Frauen* (Darmstadt: Wissenschaftliche Buchgesellschaft, 1995), pp. 3-79, esp. p. 67.

3. I mostly use the terminology of Bal, who calls the three levels 'fabula',
'story', and 'text'; Bal, *Narratology*, pp. 5-6.

4. Bal, *Narratology*, pp. 49-51.

5. Bal, *Narratology*, pp. 119-20.

deny the historically grown shape of it, but ask for the meanings of this text aside from its historical aspects.

3. *The Text: 1 Kings 14.1-18*

The story begins with the information that Abijah, the son of Jeroboam and his wife, is ill. Then follows Jeroboam's command to his wife: she should disguise herself and go to Ahijah the prophet in order to find out about the fate of her son. And so she does.[6]

> 1 At that time Abijah son of Jeroboam fell sick. 2 Jeroboam said to his wife, 'Go, disguise yourself, so that it will not be known that you are the wife of Jeroboam, and go to Shiloh; for the prophet Ahijah is there, who said of me that I should be king over this people. 3 Take with you ten loaves, some cakes, and a jar of honey, and go to him; he will tell you what shall happen to the child.' 4 Jeroboam's wife did so; she set out and went to Shiloh, and came to the house of Ahijah.

Now the scene changes. We learn that Ahijah is blind and God tells him who is coming and what he should say.

> (4) Now Ahijah could not see, for his eyes were dim because of his age. 5 But the LORD said to Ahijah, 'The wife of Jeroboam is coming to inquire of you concerning her son; for he is sick. Thus and thus you shall say to her. And when she is coming, she will have disguised herself.'

When the wife of Jeroboam arrives, Ahijah knows immediately who she is. He starts his prophetical speech.

> 6 So when Ahijah heard the sound of her feet, as she came in at the door, he said, 'Come in, wife of Jeroboam; why have you disguised yourself? For I have a heavy [message] for you.'

This speech can be divided into three distinctive parts. First, the prophet gives the woman a message for Jeroboam, announcing evil and destruction for him and his house because of his failures.

> 7 Go, tell Jeroboam, 'Thus says the LORD, the God of Israel: Because I exalted you from among the people, made you leader over my people Israel, 8 and tore the kingdom away from the house of David to give it to you; yet you have not been like my servant David, who kept my commandments and followed me with all his heart, doing only that which was right in my sight, 9 but you have done evil above all those who were before you and have gone and made for yourself other gods, and cast images, provoking me to anger, and have thrust me behind your back; 10 therefore, I will bring evil upon the house of Jeroboam. I

---

6.   Translations from the Hebrew Bible in this essay are based on the NRSV, with some modifications.

will cut off from Jeroboam every male, both bond and free in Israel, and will consume the house of Jeroboam, just as one burns up dung until it is all gone. 11 Anyone belonging to Jeroboam who dies in the city, the dogs shall eat; and anyone who dies in the open country, the birds shall eat; for the LORD has spoken'.

In the second part the prophet tells the woman in only a few sentences that the boy will die as soon as she gets home, and that all Israel will bury him and mourn for him.

12 And you, set out, go to your house. When your feet enter the city, the child shall die. 13 All Israel shall mourn for him and bury him; for he alone of Jeroboam's family shall come to the grave, because in him there is found something pleasing to the LORD, the God of Israel in the house of Jeroboam.

The third part ends the speech with a prophecy of evil for Israel in general, because of the sins of Jeroboam.

14 And the LORD will raise up for himself a king over Israel, who shall cut off the house of Jeroboam on that day, and even right now? 15 The LORD will strike Israel, as a reed is shaken in the water; he will root up Israel out of this good land that he gave to their ancestors, and scatter them beyond the river, because they have made their Asherim, provoking the LORD to anger. 16 He will give Israel up because of the sins of Jeroboam, which he sinned and which he caused Israel to commit.

After this speech the story ends quickly. Everything Ahijah had told the woman happens. The moment she gets home, the son dies and all Israel buries him and mourns him.

17 Then Jeroboam's wife set out and went away, and she came to Tirzah. As she came to the threshold of the house, the child died. 18 All Israel buried him and mourned for him, according to the word of the LORD, which he spoke by his servant the prophet Ahijah.

4. *Identity and Disguise*

Since I have decided to turn the wife of Jeroboam into the central figure of this article, it is obvious to ask the question: 'So, who is she?' Since this is a text, she is—of course—not a person, not a human being, because she is constructed within this text. I will look at her as an actant on the level of the 'fabula', then see how she is characterized on the level of the 'story' and how the latter stands in tension with the former.

First of all she is an element in the structure of the narrative. That means that on the level of the fabula she is one of the actants, that is, one of the figures that are subjects or objects of actions. And these actions constitute the events of which the fabula is made.[7]

About Jeroboam, Ahijah, and God we learn what they do and what they want. We are told their names and we can hear their voices. However, this is different concerning the wife of Jeroboam. As an actant she is as important as the others. It would not be possible just to cut her out of the events, because her actions let the story evolve. She goes to Ahijah and causes him to deliver his prophetic speech. She also goes back and thus the child dies. Like Jeroboam and Ahijah she acts, which means she holds a subject position just as they do. But we cannot see that she has any intentions of her own. Also, she has no voice, and like many other women in 1 and 2 Kings she has no name.[8] All we know about her are her family relationships: she is the wife of Jeroboam—which is almost used as a title for her—and she is the mother of Jeroboam's son, Abijah.

Nevertheless, she is more than an element in the structure of the narrative, too. On the level of the 'story' all actants are characterized by the way they act and the circumstances in which they act. This is the way the actants are seen in the 'story' and presented to the readers.[9] The reader is given more detailed information about Jeroboam and Ahijah through Jeroboam's intention to question the prophet, and within Ahijah's speech. Ahijah is a prophet close to God, from whom he gets his information. Furthermore, he is blind. Jeroboam is a king whose future had been foretold by this prophet, who is condemning him now because he did wrong against God. Nothing is told about the wife of Jeroboam which would make her distinguishable. As shown above, she does not even have a name. Thus, all this would hint towards the conclusion that, as a character, she is not especially

---

7.   Bal, *Narratology*, p. 5.

8.   At first it seems unnecessary to mention that, like so many others, the woman does not have a name (e.g. the widow of Zarephath in 1 Kgs 17.8-24; the woman Elisha approaches in 2 Kgs 4.1-7; the Shunammite woman in 2 Kgs 4.8-37, 8.1-6). But her namelessness is symptomatic of the position of women in 1 and 2 Kings. A. Reinhartz points out that the anonymity of women in 1 and 2 Kings is used as a narrative technique to focus the attention of the reader towards the type the woman represents and towards the named, male, central figure; A. Reinhartz, 'Anonymous Women and the Collapse of the Monarchy: A Study in Narrative Technique', in A. Brenner (ed.), *A Feminist Companion to Samuel and Kings* (Sheffield: Sheffield Academic Press, 1994), pp. 43-65.

9.   On characterization in narratives see Bal, *Narratology*, pp. 79-93 and A. Berlin, *Poetics and Interpretation in Biblical Narrative* (Bible and Literature, 9; Sheffield: Almond Press, 1983), esp. ch. 2, 'Character and Characterization', pp. 23-42.

necessary; in other words, any other actant could have done her 'job'.

However, there are features in the narrative that speak against this suggestion. Jeroboam addresses *her* and sends *her*, not just any servant, and he tells her: '*Go, disguise yourself, so that it will not be known that you are the wife of Jeroboam…*' (v. 2). This is the first hint that, in the story, the wife of Jeroboam has something like what we would call today 'an identity'. This identity seems to be important enough that it needs to be hidden, even from a blind man; and furthermore, it is important enough for God to tell Ahijah about it beforehand: '*The wife of Jeroboam is coming to inquire of you concerning her son; for he is sick. Thus and thus you shall say to her. And when she is coming, she will have disguised herself*' (v. 5). So when she enters Ahijah's house, *he* addresses her by her name or title: '*Come in, Wife of Jeroboam*' (v. 6)—to show that he already knows who she is. All this leads to the conclusion that she is not just an actant who could be exchanged with any other actant, such as a servant. At any rate, there seems to be at least one reason why she has to be her husband's messenger. She is the wife of Jeroboam, and acting on his behalf and in his interest: *he* sends her with *his* question to the prophet that had foretold *his* future as a king. And Ahijah starts out with a message for *him*, and ends with one about the fate of the people Israel, caused *by* him. So, in this respect, the woman is not the figure who could be substituted, yet already she *is* the substitute for Jeroboam, the king.

If this assumption is right, then the story does not show Jeroboam in a very favorable light. It is not outstandingly virtuous for a king to send someone else to hear God's word of judgment upon himself. One explanation why Jeroboam himself is not going to Ahijah might be the tendency in the narrative to describe Jeroboam in a disapproving way.[10]

But not all the message is for Jeroboam, and the whole business is not only his. It is also *her* son, for whose fate she is asking. And the answer to this question Ahijah addresses to her directly: '*Therefore, set out, go to your house. When your feet enter the city, the child shall die*' (v. 12). The woman, as the mother of Abijah, is the recipient of this message, and the one with whom the death of the child is connected. I

10. The negative tendency in the judgment about Jeroboam can be found in the stereotypical deuteronomistic formulas all through the following chapters of Kings, where the sins of Jeroboam, and the sins Jeroboam caused Israel to commit, are mentioned again and again as a reproach against other kings of Israel; see, for example, 1 Kgs 15.30; 16.31; 2 Kgs 3.3. Cf. E. Würthwein, *Die Bücher der Könige 1: Könige 17–2. Könige 25* (ATD 11.2; Göttingen: Vandenhoeck & Ruprecht, 1984), p. 492.

therefore claim that again, in this respect, the woman cannot be substituted.[11]

So I take for granted that the wife of Jeroboam is indispensable not only as an actant, but also as a character. She is not exchangeable *because* she is the wife of Jeroboam and *because* she is the mother of Abijah. One also gets the impression that she has an identity behind the disguise, an identity that would not allow just anybody to be sent. Thus, in terms of social roles, the woman's identity behind the disguise is that of a wife and mother.[12] While looking for her as a character beyond these roles, her disguise is all one can find. Only the command to make herself unrecognizable gives the reader the impression that, undisguised, she would be a distinct character, a 'real' woman. But one can see that this is only an illusion. First of all, there are never 'real women' in the text but, as I have argued above, only textually constructed women. Even beyond this, the woman is actually uncovered in the story so that the reader does not have to continue wondering what is behind the mask: informed by God, Ahijah recognizes her. But this has no impact on the way the story lets her seem to be a non-person, an actant but not a character.[13] Therefore, it is even more important to look for structures of representation—because this technique of disguise is a structure—and not for 'real' biblical women; after all, there is no 'real' woman in the text. The closest to 'real' we can get is the woman in disguise, and the woman in her social roles as wife and mother.

11.   There is a type of 'mother-with-sick-child (esp. son)' in the narratives of 1 and 2 Kgs (e.g. 1 Kgs 17.17-24; 2 Kgs 4.18-37). A type is a character, with certain stereotypical traits, that stands for a whole group. Cf. A. Berlin, *Poetics*, p. 32. Comparing the different stories in 1 and 2 Kings where this type is employed, and considering the deviations from it, will probably give other interesting insights into the story. However, I will deal with this elsewhere (in my dissertation on women in Kings). Reinhartz has dealt with this in part within the section about 'Mothers and Prophets' in her article about anonymous women in Kings (Reinhartz, 'Anonymous Women', pp. 56-60).

12.   Of course, since this is a text, social roles are also literary roles here. Usually, for women, these were in the realm of the family because this was 'considered normative for a decent woman'; A. Brenner, *The Israelite Woman: Social Role and Literary Type in Biblical Narrative* (Sheffield: JSOT Press, 1985), p. 91.

13.   Here I do not agree with Reinhartz, who sees in the disguise—even for a blind man—the 'complete self-effacement' of the woman ('Anonymous Women', p. 59). I do not think that this is *self*-effacement but, rather, that the men of the story together with the narrator take part in presenting her as a non-person.

5. 'House' and 'House'

Another aspect of narrative texts is the question of place and space. Usually in a narrative there are places where the events happen. The places of this story are the house of Jeroboam in Tirzah and the house of Ahijah in Shiloh. Naming these places belongs to the level of the 'fabula'.[14]

On the level of the 'story' the different places are shown in relation to each other. In this way, space is created in the narrative.[15] Here, the two men stay in their houses, and it is the woman who connects these places and opens up the space by going back and forth between them. But although she is the one who constitutes the space in the story, there is no place left for her in the end. When she enters the house of Ahijah she is 'dis-covered' in the true sense of the word by the knowledge Ahijah has received from God, and is told a heavy message. Her experiences there do not make the house of Ahijah a safe place for her.

Furthermore, in speaking to her Ahijah also turns her own house for her into a place of death, too. He connects her coming home with the death of her son, which is what happens eventually: She *'set out and went away, and she came to Tirzah. As she came to the threshold of the house, the child died'* (v. 17). Therefore, the threshold that separates the outside world from her house is also the threshold between life and death for her son. The message Ahijah gives her, *'Therefore, I will bring evil upon the house of Jeroboam...'* (v. 10), is about the total destruction of the house of Jeroboam, which is the family she belongs to as well.[16] And thus, the message tells her that she will also lose her house, meaning her family and probably her life.

Even on the level of the 'text' it becomes obvious that she has no place, because the questions 'Who speaks?' and 'To whom?' reveal that this message is for Jeroboam, and is only sent *through* her, but not addressed *to* her. So she is told the news of her family's end, including her own end, as a message for someone else.

14. Bal, *Narratology*, p. 43.
15. Bal, *Narratology*, p. 93.
16. 'House' in terms of 'family' usually includes the parents and their sons, possibly with their families, and the unmarried daughters; S. Bendor, *The Social Structure of Ancient Israel* (Jerusalem: Simor, 1996), pp. 48-53. Additionally, the house of a king has a dynastic aspect. Thus the king's 'house' covers 'family' as well as national matters. The private and the political cannot be separated here, even less so than usual. Cf. I. Müllner, *Gewalt im Hause Davids: Die Erzählung von Tamar und Amnon (2 Sam 13,1-22)* (HBS, 13; Freiburg: Herder, 1997), p. 130.

In the end, the woman has no place at all that does not mean death and terror. Even her own death does not have a place. Abijah, the son, is buried *'by all Israel'* (v. 18). Jeroboam dies and, contrary to Ahijah's words, is buried with his ancestors—which means he has a place even after his death. 1 Kgs 15.29 says that Ba'asha destroyed the house of Jeroboam. But the fate of the wife of Jeroboam is not reported. She just disappears.

6. *Where is God?*

Another way of looking at the position of the wife of Jeroboam in the story is to ask for her relations to other actants. I am going to look at a special set of relationships now by asking: where is God in the story? How are the different actants connected to God? Looking for answers to this question will show that the quality of the different relations to God is one of the main topics of the story.[17]

We have already seen that Ahijah is closely connected to God—which is not very surprising since he is a prophet. He gets his information from God, who exposes the identity of the wife of Jeroboam before Ahijah. And God tells him the words he is to speak. In this way he is Jeroboam's connection to God. We learn in the text that Ahijah is known to Jeroboam because he is the prophet *'who said of me that I should be king over this people'* (v. 2). Asking the same prophet about the child also means asking if God still favors Jeroboam. And the answer God gives through Ahijah is clearly negative: God will *'bring evil upon the house of Jeroboam'* (v. 10) and *'will give Israel up because of the sins of Jeroboam...'* (v. 16). In the same speech Ahijah reveals what kind of relationship Abijah, the son, has to God. Ahijah speaks about him: *'All Israel shall mourn for him and bury him; for he alone of Jeroboam's family shall come to the grave, because in him there is found something pleasing to the LORD, the God of Israel, in the house of Jeroboam'* (v. 13). So, all male characters in the story are, in one way or another, connected with God. The God of this story belongs to the male actants in the narrative while the wife of Jeroboam is sent, is exposed, and is sent back. Only the wife of Jeroboam is not at all connected to God. The message about the destruction of the house of Jeroboam is sent *through* her, but is not addressed *to* her. And the part of Ahijah's message for her is the

---

17. I agree with Bal that one of the strengths of narratological analysis is that God is treated like any other character in the narrative, 'which allows a narratological analysis to become truly critical'; Bal, *Death and Dissymmetry: The Politics of Coherence in the Book of Judges* (Chicago: University of Chicago Press, 1988), p. 34.

only part where he neither speaks explicitly in the name of God, nor about God.

It is interesting—even though not very surprising—that the relationships of the actants to God are mostly communicated on the level of the 'text'. They are issues of 'Who speaks to whom and about whom?'. The reason for this is mostly that God's presence in the narrative is not visible; rather, God's presence is revealed through communication. This observation corresponds with the fact that the woman has no voice; therefore, she is not able to take an active part in the discourse about relations to God—and, as we have seen, nobody speaks to her about it, either. Since the wife of Jeroboam does not have a relationship with God, there is, alone among the characters, no God for her to whom she can turn.

7. Summary

After looking at the story about the wife of Jeroboam from three different angles, I will give a short summary of what we have found.

On the level of the 'fabula', she is one of the central figures, because her actions are important for the course of events. Still, she has no name and no intentions.

On the level of the 'story', she is presented as one who has no place in the end. Her identity as a character is constructed through the disguise. Behind it, we can see her in her social roles as wife and mother, but it makes no sense to try to search any further. There is no 'real' woman behind those roles. Her identity lies in the illusion that without the disguise she would be someone recognizable and remembered. Thus, it is through the disguise that a position at the center and at the fringe is constructed.

On the level of the 'text', she stands outside the discourse about the various kinds of relations to God, and therefore has no God to whom she can turn.

Therefore, as I have claimed, the wife of Jeroboam is presented differently on each level of the narratological analysis. The contradictory images of her at the center and at the margins produce an ambivalent position.

8. Women in 1 and 2 Kings—Center or Fringe?

I started out with the proposition that the wife of Jeroboam is, simultaneously, positioned on the margins and at the center of the narrative. Looking at additional narratives with female characters in the books of Kings we can see, on the formal level, the same ambivalence in their position in the composition of the books as a whole.

Ironically, on the content level in the books of Kings, women other than the wife of Jeroboam are often among the main characters of their stories.[18] However, in 1 and 2 Kings history is constructed through a framework of kings and prophets—almost all of them male[19]—following one after another, dealing with issues of government, war and peace, and of God and other gods.[20] The stories in which women are at the center usually do not belong to that line of events. And if they do, it is because of the male central figures in the text, such as Jeroboam and Ahijah in 1 Kings 14. Therefore, even if women are at the center of their stories, they get marginalized by the framework of history that is presented in the books of Kings. Thus, whether their position is on the fringe or at the center depends on how their stories are read and from which angle they are viewed.

Mieke Bal introduced the concept of 'countercoherences'[21] in her study of the book of Judges. She argues that presuppositions about the main topic of a book in its reception constitute a certain kind of coherence, which for Judges is usually the coherence of chronological political and military history. All stories that do not fit into this line are eliminated from the coherence. Against this Bal poses her concept of countercoherence in Judges, a concept that has its starting point not with the heroes and the victories, but with the victims and the loss; not with the men, but with the women:

> A countercoherence relates the 'official' reading to what it leaves out; it relates the texts to the needs of the reader; it relates everything that is denied importance to the motivations for such denials. The countercoherence will start precisely where repression is the most flagrant.

---

18. Almost all the women who appear in narratives in 1 and 2 Kings are main characters in these stories, e.g. the widow from Zarephath in 1 Kgs 17.8-24, Jezebel in 1 Kgs 21 and 2 Kgs 9.30-37, the Shunammite woman in 2 Kgs 4.8-37 and 8.1-6, and more.

19. Exceptions are the queen Athaliah (2 Kgs 11) and the prophetess Huldah (2 Kgs 22).

20. This concept of history in Kings is usually attributed to deuteronomic history; see Würthwein, *Bücher der Könige*, pp. 504-505. For a critical discussion of the concept of deuteronomic history see H.N. Rösel, *Von Josua bis Jojachin: Untersuchungen zu den deuteronomistischen Geschichtsbüchern im Alten Testament* (VTSup, 75; Leiden: E.J. Brill, 1999). But even if the construction of this framework is redactional and, therefore, center and fringe positions had occurred at different diachronic stages, this would not solve the tension between the two poles in the text as it exists today.

21. Bal, *Death*, p. 20.

Since men are said to lead the game, I will start with the women; since
conquest is said to be the issue, I will start with loss; since strength is
said to be the major asset of the characters, I will start with the victims.[22]

Looking at the women in 1 and 2 Kings in a different way gives the
opportunity to set up such countercoherence.

By way of conclusion, I will give another picture to illustrate this
kind of change of perspective. Some of you might know the kind of
drawing-game that you can find on the children's page of certain
magazines. What you see there is a square with a lot of dots, each
having a number. In order to make the dots into a picture you have to
draw a line from one dot to the next according to their numbers, in an
ascending order, from 1 to 2 to 3 and so on. In the end the lines build
the picture of a king, for example. In our case the dots of 1 and 2
Kings are numbered in a certain way, so that the picture being formed
is that of history as a line of men—kings and prophets. The dots of the
women's stories are integrated *somewhere* in the picture, but some of
them might not even have a number at all. If we want to get the
women from the fringe to the center, we would have to give new
numbers to the dots, so that the line would be drawn in a different
way and, in the end, the emerging picture would be a different
picture. It could be the picture of several fairly diverse women, most
of them struggling for life, for their own and often for the life of their
children, some of them turning to prophets or kings for help, and
some of them reaching for the power to rule by themselves. Yet all of
them would be an integral part of the people of Israel and Judah in
building their history with God.

22. Bal, *Death*, p.17.

THE WIDOW OF ZAREPHATH
AND THE GREAT WOMAN OF SHUNEM:
A COMPARATIVE ANALYSIS OF TWO STORIES[*]

Jopie Siebert-Hommes

Fokkelien van Dijk-Hemmes has deepened the research of the Hebrew
Bible significantly by giving a place to feminist literary criticism within biblical exegesis.

The gender-specific method of reading the Bible, as developed and
applied by van Dijk-Hemmes, enables the exegete critically to examine the Bible story and to lay bare the literary strategies in the text.
Derived from the narratological theory of Mieke Bal, this method
poses questions concerning the narrative composition of the text, such
as: Who is speaking? Who is seeing? Who is acting? Which objectives
are pursued by the different characters in the text?[1]

One of the most striking examples of the application of this method
is offered by van Dijk-Hemmes in her study on the prophet Elisha and
the 'great woman' of Shunem (2 Kgs 4.8-37).[2] She presents a 'dual
hermeneutic' of this story, that is, she offers both a negative critical interpretation and a positive critical interpretation.[3] In the negative critical interpretation she lays bare the patriarchal structures of the text

---

    [*]   First published in Bob Becking and Meindert Dijkstra (eds.), *On Reading
Prophetic Texts: Gender-Specific and Related Studies in Memory of Fokkelien van Dijk-
Hemmes* (Leiden: E.J. Brill, 1996), pp. 231-50. Reprinted with permission.

    1.   Cf. Fokkelien van Dijk-Hemmes, *Sporen van vrouwenteksten in de Hebreeuwse
Bijbel* (Utrechtse Theologische Reeks, 16; Utrecht: Universiteit Utrecht, 1992), p. 56.
For a survey of narratological principles see Mieke Bal, *Narratology: Introduction to
the Theory of Narrative* (Toronto: Toronto University Press, 1985).

    2.   Fokkelien van Dijk-Hemmes, 'The Great Woman of Shunem and the Man
of God: A Dual Interpretation of 2 Kings 4.8-37', in Athalya Brenner (ed.), *A Feminist Companion to Samuel and Kings* (Feminist Companion to the Bible, 5; Sheffield:
Sheffield Academic Press, 1994), pp. 218-30.

    3.   Van Dijk-Hemmes was inspired by the ideas of Patricinio Schweickart.
Cf. 'Reading Ourselves: Toward a Feminist Theory of Reading', in E.A. Flynn and
P. Schweickart (eds.), *Gender and Reading: Essays on Readers, Texts and Contexts*
(Baltimore: The Johns Hopkins University Press, 1986), pp. 31-62.

and thereby exposes the complicity of this text in the patriarchal ideology: 'Our story can, it seems, be interpreted as an extraordinary feast of patriarchal propaganda'.[4] The fact that the patriarchal order has to be promoted so emphatically indicates that this order is not a matter of course: the patriarchal order needs continual reaffirmation and the text contains a literary strategy supporting this affirmation. Van Dijk-Hemmes tries to trace this literary strategy in order to be able to look beyond the patriarchal wrappings of the message.

After unmasking the strategy, she searches for the positive critical hermeneutic which recovers and focuses on the universally shared ideals from which this text derives a significant portion of its emotional eloquence. In a profound and fascinating analysis, van Dijk-Hemmes shows that the way Elisha is presented in this story is coloured by irony. The portrait of Elisha is entirely different in this respect to that of his predecessor Elijah. According to van Dijk-Hemmes, 'The stories about Elisha seem to be parodic offshoots of stories about Elijah. The same narrated events are recounted in a grotesque way.'[5] That the story of Elisha in 2 Kgs 4.8-37 could be a parody on the story of Elijah in 1 Kgs 17.8-24 is an intriguing presupposition worthy of further research. Following the article by van Dijk-Hemmes I would, therefore, like to elaborate on the parallels between the two stories and investigate further their similarities and differences. My attention is particularly focused on the role of the main characters and their place in the literary composition of the text.

Two Stories

The first similarity between the two stories has to do with the main characters: in both cases these are a prophet of YHWH, a woman and the woman's son. In both stories, the prophet has an upper room with a bed in the home of the woman who provides him with his daily bread. In both stories, the son becomes ill and dies, whereupon the woman turns reproachfully to the prophet. The child is laid on the prophet's bed and the prophet prays to YHWH, after which the prophet stretches himself upon the body of the child in a type of magical ritual.[6] The child revives and the prophet gives him back to his mother. Particularly remarkable is the fact that both women give an identical testimony concerning the prophet.

4. Van Dijk-Hemmes, 'The Great Woman', p. 227.
5. Van Dijk-Hemmes, 'The Great Woman', p. 228.
6. In other ancient Near Eastern texts comparable rituals occur. Cf. Bob Becking, *Een magisch ritueel in Jahwistisch perspectief: 2 Kon. 4.31-38* (Utrechtse Theolo-

What are the roles of the three main characters? Who speaks and what does each person say? Who acts in these stories and from whose point of view is the story told?

Story 1

The prophet in story 1 is called 'Elijah, the Tishbite' who comes from 'Tishbe in Gilead', on the other side of the Jordan.[7] There is no record of his calling to be a prophet; he is not even introduced as a prophet.[8] Without warning, he appears on the stage, saying concerning himself that he 'stands before the face of YHWH, the God of Israel' (1 Kgs 17.1). The text reports that 'the word of YHWH came to him' (vv. 2, 8) and that 'Elijah does according to the word of YHWH' (v. 5).

Elijah's performance begins with the announcement to Ahab of the coming great drought (1 Kgs 17.1). Thereafter, he is sent by the word of YHWH to the brook Cherith, where the ravens bring him food and where he can drink from the brook. When the brook dries up, the word of YHWH sends him to Zarephath where a woman, a widow, will provide for him. The ravens and the widow take care of Elijah at YHWH's command (vv. 4, 9). These circumstances are remarkable because both ravens and widows belong to a category towards which God's own merciful kindness is needed.[9] In this story, on the contrary, the opposite occurs: at YHWH's command the ravens and the widow are to care mercifully for the prophet.

After a while, YHWH instructs Elijah to make his appearance again and present himself to Ahab with a proclamation: YHWH will once more send rain (1 Kgs 18.1). In this manner, the story of the ravens and the widow is enclosed within a chiasmus:

no rain / disappearance (17.1-3)
reappearance / rain again (18.1)

gische Reeks, 17; Utrecht: Universiteit Utrecht, 1992). Becking draws attention to the connection between prayer and gesture in the story of Elisha (2 Kgs 4). In his opinion, both elements—prayer and gesture—belong to the oldest layer in the story (see p. 26).

7.   Elijah is an outsider in most senses of the term. Cf. Wesley J. Bergen, 'The Prophetic Alternative: Elisha and the Israelite Monarchy', in Robert B. Coote (ed.), *Elijah and Elisha in Socioliterary Perspective* (Atlanta: Scholars Press, 1992), pp. 127-38 (p. 136).

8.   The LXX adds the epithet 'the prophet' in 17.1.

9.   In the Bible the raven is known as a bird of prey (Isa. 34.11; Prov. 30.17), but also as a bird whose young are fed by YHWH (Ps. 147.9; Job 38.41). It is precisely this bird that is commissioned by YHWH to feed Elijah.

The story (17.4-24) within this framework answers the question of whether the 'word of YHWH' from the mouth of the prophet is trust-worthy. This question is important in view of the following story, the impressive happenings on Mt Carmel (1 Kgs 18), where it will be manifested who the true God is: Baal or YHWH.

The story about the ravens and the widow is the introduction to the momentous story which follows. In this introduction it will be affirmed that it is Elijah the prophet in whose mouth the word of YHWH is trustworthy.[10] In the literary composition of the text, the theme becomes clear: the expression 'the word of YHWH' has a strik-ing place in the structure.[11]

```
framework: YHWH—no rain (17.1)
      WORD of YHWH (comes to Elijah) (2)
            Cherith / Jordan (3)
            brook / ravens (4)
      WORD of YHWH (executed by Elijah) (5a)
            Cherith / Jordan (5b)
            ravens / brook (6)
            no rain (7)
      WORD of YHWH (comes to Elijah) (8)
            Zarephath / widow (2×) (9,10a)
            water / bread (for Elijah) (10b,11)
                  no bread = death (12)
                        YHWH gives meal and oil (14a)
                        YHWH gives rain (14b)
                  answer to prayer = life (15,16a)
      WORD of YHWH (spoken through Elijah) (16b)
            son ill = death (17)
            reproach to the man of God (18)
                  upper room—ascent (19)
                        to YHWH: prayer for the widow (20)
                              Elijah stretches himself out (21a)
                        to YHWH: prayer for the son (21b)
                              answer to prayer (22)
                  upper room—descent (23)
            son living = life (23b)
            testimony: you man of God (24a)
      WORD of YHWH (in Elijah's mouth is trustworthy) (24b)
framework: YHWH—rain (18.1)
```

10. It is 'disclosed' that Elijah the Tishbite, a stranger, is the servant of YHWH: 'le programme principal qui sous-tend ce récit est un DEVOILEMENT'. Cf. M.L. Fabre and A. Geuret, 'Elie et la veuve de Sarepta: Analyse sémiotique de I. Rois 17', *Sémiotique et Bible* 14 (1979), pp. 2-14 (p. 9).

11. Structure has rhetorical and expressive value. 'It is one of the factors governing the effect of the work on the reader and in addition it serves to express or accentuate meaning'; so S. Bar-Efrat, 'Some Observations on the Analysis of Structure in Biblical Narrative', *VT* 30 (1980), pp. 154-73 (p. 172).

The expression 'word of YHWH' occurs five times in this story, each time in relation to Elijah (vv. 2, 5, 8, 16, 24). The last verse in which the expression occurs is, simultaneously, also the conclusion of the story (v. 4):

> A man of God are you
> the word of YHWH in your mouth
> is trustworthy.[12]

The woman pronounces this conclusion; nonetheless, she knew from the start who the God of Elijah was, for in her first words she speaks of him: 'By the life of YHWH, your God' (v. 12). These words echo the first words which Elijah spoke to Ahab: 'By the life of YHWH, the God of Israel' (v. 1). The conclusion, 'the word of YHWH in *your mouth* is trustworthy', also contains an allusion to Elijah's speech to Ahab in which he spoke of 'the word of *my mouth*' (17.1).

The Relation between the Prophet and the Woman
The encounter between the prophet and the woman radiates empathy and understanding. At their first meeting, Elijah asks with modesty and deference for a 'little water' (v. 10). Then, when the woman walks away, he asks for a 'morsel of bread' (v. 11). The addition 'in your hand' suggests that he intends a small piece of bread, again emphasizing his modesty. When the woman refuses his request because she has nothing to give (v. 12), he puts her mind at ease: 'Fear not' (v. 13), followed by a detailed description of what she is to do. The prophet reiterates the words of the woman but alters them slightly, thus delineating clearly his prophetic manner of operation. The changes reveal that things will go differently from the way the woman assumes them to go.

The woman says: 'I have no bread-cake'.
Elijah answers: 'Make a bread-cake first for me'.

The woman says: 'I have only a handful of flour and a bit of oil'.
Elijah answers: 'The flour shall not run out and the oil will not diminish'.

The last words of the woman, 'We shall eat and die' (v. 12) are, however, not repeated by Elijah. Instead he refers to the rain which YHWH will send upon the earth (v. 14). The mention of 'death' is not repeated by Elijah, but neither does he speak of 'life', as one perhaps might expect. Yet, Elijah's mention of 'rain' (v. 14) does contain a *reference* to

12. The translations of Bible texts in this article are mine; I have followed the Hebrew text as closely as possible.

'life'. It refers indirectly to the 'life' which YHWH will give,[13] not only to the woman and her son but also to all of Israel. The promise Elijah here pronounces reaches beyond this story to the following chapter (1 Kgs 18), where the word of YHWH proclaims 'rain upon the earth' (18.1). This rain means 'life' to Israel both literally and figuratively. Literally, rain means the end of drought and famine. But the figurative aspect is even more important, for Israel shall know that YHWH is 'God' and that Elijah, the prophet, is his servant (18.36).

It is surprising that it is a woman who expresses with so many words the identity of Elijah (v. 24). She is but a woman, and a widow at that, which means that she is a non-entity in a patriarchal religious society. In addition, she comes from Zarephath in Sidon: she is not even an Israelite woman.[14] The text, nonetheless, places the witness of Elijah's legitimacy precisely in her mouth. Seen from this perspective, it is even more amazing that, concerning herself, the woman speaks of 'sins'. She says to Elijah (v. 18):

> Man of God, have you come to me
> to bring my sins to remembrance?

Scholars assume that the woman had committed some obscure sin: 'Such a state was considered incompatible with the divine presence, of which the spirit in the man of God was the extension'.[15] From the reaction of Elijah, however, one cannot conclude that he takes the illness of the child as divine punishment for some sin not yet expiated. On the contrary: 'Give me your son', he says to the woman, and he lays the boy upon his own bed. His ensuing prayer is in the first place for the widow: not mentioning her sins, he emphasizes her hospitality. It is as though he asks God: are you really at the right address with this heavy punishment? Why do you strike this woman, who has shown me such hospitality, with so great a calamity by letting her son die?

Both Elijah (v. 20) and the woman (v. 18) ask about the 'why' of this

---

13. I agree with Robinson: 'All the stories told of Elijah in this chapter have been chosen to illustrate one point, that Yahweh and not Baal was the giver of life'. Cf. J. Robinson, *The First Book of Kings* (Cambridge: Cambridge University Press, 1972), p. 203.

14. In other Bible texts as well, Sidon is a 'heathen' city. Cf. 1 Kgs 16.31: the king of the Sidonians was the father of Jezebel. And see Judg. 1.31, where the Sidonians belong to those who actually should have been driven out after the settlement.

15. John Gray, *I and II Kings: A Commentary* (OTL; Philadelphia: Westminster Press, 1964; 2nd edn; London: SCM Press, 1977), p. 382.

death. There is, however, a contrast in contents: while the woman refers to her sins, Elijah refers to her hospitality and does not relate the death of the boy to some possible sin.

Jezebel

Some commentators suggest that the widow in this story is sketched in striking contrast to the other Sidonian woman in the Elijah cycle, Jezebel.[16] Jezebel is a propagator of the Baal cult (1 Kgs 16.31). Like the widow, she too gives nourishment to prophets, that is, to the prophets of Baal and Asherah (1 Kgs 18.19), but she eradicates the prophets of YHWH (1 Kgs 18.4, 13). When confronted with the stories of the actions of Elijah, she does not admit that Elijah is a man of God, but attempts to kill him (1 Kgs 19.1).[17] Later on, the opposite to what happened to the widow of Zarephath befalls Jezebel: Jezebel's son Ahaziah becomes ill after falling from an 'upper room' (2 Kgs 1.2). Elijah does not come to this upper room to raise him up from the bed on which he lies (2 Kgs 1.16); instead, from his mouth sounds the 'word of YHWH' that Ahaziah will die.

The contrasting parallels between the widow of Zarephath and Queen Jezebel clarify the problematic text in 1 Kgs 17.18, where the text implicitly refers to the other Sidonian woman, Jezebel. It is not the sins of the widow but the sins of the other woman which will later be 'brought to remembrance': her son will die.

Story 2

The prophet in story 2 is Elisha. The story again seems to be about the legitimacy of the prophet, and again it is a woman who confirms the legitimacy by her words. As already mentioned, she uses words that are almost identical to the words of the woman in the first story. The surprising element is that the woman in the second story does this immediately at the beginning of the story:

I know
this is a (holy) man of God (2 Kgs 4.9).

16. Cf. K.A.D. Smelik, 'The Literary Function of 1 Kgs 17,8-24', in C. Brekelmans and J. Lust (eds.), *Pentateuchal and Deuteronomistic Studies* (Leuven: Peeters, 1990), pp. 239-43 (p. 241).

17. Athalya Brenner is right in observing that 'the YHWH–Baal conflict is, in fact, not the story of Elijah versus Ahab...but of Jezebel versus Elijah'. Cf. Athalya Brenner, *The Israelite Woman: Social Role and Literary Type in Biblical Narrative* (Sheffield: Sheffield Academic Press, 2nd edn, 1994), p. 28.

Elisha, a Man of God?

The appellation 'man of God' occurs eight times in this story, three times from the mouth of the woman (vv. 9, 16, 22). Twice she speaks to her husband about the 'man of God' (vv. 9, 22) and once she addresses Elisha himself with this title, namely, when he promises her a son (v. 16). Here she uses the double appellation: 'my lord, man of God'. When the woman later comes to the prophet after the death of her son, she does *not* address him as 'man of God', but only as 'my lord' (v. 28). Shortly before this, however, the appellation 'man of God' sounded five times in the description of what happened from the moment that the boy died until Elisha was informed about the fact:

> She laid him on the bed of the *man of God* (v. 21).
> She came to the *man of God* (v. 25a).
> The *man of God* saw the Shunammite (v. 25b).
> She came to the *man of God* (v. 27a).
> The *man of God* said: her soul is bitter (v. 27b).

Is there perhaps some irony in this repetition of the epithet? The tension mounts as the question becomes more urgent as to whether Elisha will indeed manifest himself as the 'man of God'. For the woman it is not really an issue: she lays her child on the bed of the man of God and runs to him.

What are Elisha's own thoughts concerning himself as a 'man of God'? He sits on Mt Carmel (v. 25)[18] but what he is doing there remains unclear. What is his actual relationship to his 'Commissioner'? He admits that YHWH has not communicated to him concerning the bitter course of events (v. 27). What is even more strange is that though the woman runs to him, he does not move to meet her. He does not speak to her, but only sends his servant to inquire concerning her שלום (v. 26). The woman gives the servant an evasive answer, but to Elisha she makes it clear that something terrible has happened. Even then the prophet remains seated and merely sends his servant to the boy to awaken him by means of Elisha's staff (v. 29). The woman

---

18. After Elijah was taken up, Elisha went back the way they had first gone together: via the Jordan, Jericho and Bethel to Mt Carmel (2 Kgs 2.13, 15, 23, 25). In many texts Mt Carmel is merely a mountain among other mountains, but for Elijah Mt Carmel played an important role: upon Mt Carmel it became clear how foolish Baal's prophets were (1 Kgs 18). Cf. also 1 Sam. 15.12: Saul's failure was upon Carmel. And cf. Nabal, the fool, who lived and worked in Carmel: 1 Sam. 25.2 (×2), 5, 7, 40.

takes the 'man of God' seriously, in any case. She ignores the servant and appeals to the prophet's responsibility (v. 30):

> By the life of YHWH
> and by the life of your soul
> I shall not leave you.

These words remind the prophet of his calling. These same words he had uttered himself (thrice!) to Elijah when the latter was about to be taken up into heaven. Elijah had tried to convince Elisha not to follow him, but Elisha had persevered, saying (2 Kgs 2.2, 4, 6):

> By the life of YHWH
> and by the life of your soul
> I shall not leave you.

Thus had Elisha become Elijah's successor. Now spoken by the Shunammite, these words make Elisha arise. He *follows* her, literally and figuratively. Will the woman bring Elisha back to his calling as 'man of God'? The staff of Elisha in the hand of Gehazi is not able to arouse the boy (v. 31). The performance and prayers of the prophet himself are necessary. Just as he himself earlier had been tenacious with Elijah, so the woman is now persistent. Van Dijk-Hemmes writes: 'Thanks to the persistence and actions of the "Great Woman", Elisha proves to be a man of God and the child is brought back to life'.[19]

Elisha's calling is important. In contrast to Elijah, the story of the calling of Elisha is preserved in the book of the Kings. Elisha is sketched as the successor to Elijah, YHWH himself gave the commission (1 Kgs 19.16):

> You shall anoint Elisha
> to be prophet in your stead.[20]

On that occasion, Elijah threw him his prophet's mantle. Later, when Elijah was to be taken up to heaven, Elisha is again thrown the prophet's mantle (2 Kgs 2.13). He strikes the waters of the Jordan with it (2.14) just as Elijah before him had done (2.8), and the waters yield.[21] 'The spirit of Elijah rests upon him', observe the sons of the

---

19. Van Dijk-Hemmes, 'The Great Woman', p. 229.

20. It is remarkable that Elisha is anointed. The anointing of kings, priests and holy objects is quite customary, but Elisha is the only one who is ordained as a prophet in this manner.

21. There are parallels here with the story of Moses. The same is true of the following pericope, where the waters of Jericho are healed (2 Kgs 2.19-22); cf. the water-sweetening story at Marah (Exod. 15.23-25). See Dorothy Irvin, 'The Joseph and Moses Stories as Narrative in the Light of Ancient Near Eastern Narrative', in

prophets (2.15). Nonetheless, the ensuing stories exhibit some peculiar characteristics. The most disturbing story is the one in which Elisha is mocked by a group of boys. He curses the boys and forty-two of them perish (2.23-25). His behaviour towards the Shunammite is also astonishing.

The Relation between the Prophet and the Woman
It is conspicuous that the contact between Elisha and the woman occurs almost exclusively through the mediation of Gehazi.[22] Thrice Elisha lets his servant call the woman, each time with the same choice of words (vv. 12, 15, 36):

> Call the Shunammite
> and he called her.

When she appears, Elisha does not address her directly but instructs Gehazi to convey his question to her. When promising her a son, Elisha addresses her for the first time personally. Her reaction, however, is a renouncement (v. 16):

> No, my lord, man of God
> do not deceive your maidservant.

The widow in story 1 also had difficulty believing the words of the prophet. Elijah reacted sympathetically and reassured her, saying 'fear not' (1 Kgs 17.13). In contrast, Elisha in story 2 ignores the negative reaction of the woman. After conveying his message, he holds his peace. In a later scene, when the woman comes to him after the son has died, the prophet addresses himself not to her but to Gehazi (vv. 25-27, 29). The woman herself confronts the prophet reproachfully (v. 28):

> Did I ask my lord for a son?
> Did I not say:
> Do not entice me to false hope?

John H. Hayes and J. Maxwell Miller (eds.), *Israelite and Judean History* (London: SCM Press, 1977), pp. 180-202 (197).
22. 'Despite the woman's impeccable conduct and profound piety, Elisha continues to refer to her as "the Shunamite" and sometimes with the more derisive "that Shunamite" (v. 25), as if he never condescended to learn her name'. Cf. Esther Fuchs, 'The Literary Characterization of Mothers and Sexual Politics in the Hebrew Bible', in Adela Yarbro Collins (ed.), *Feminist Perspectives on Biblical Scholarship* (Chico, CA: Scholars Press, 1985), pp. 117-36 (128).

Elisha does not answer her but, rather, gives Gehazi some instructions without concerning himself with the desperate woman. Why does Elisha not address the woman directly? Why does he so specifically seek the mediation of Gehazi? Even after the revival of the son, the contact is at first channelled through Gehazi. The latter is to call the woman and, when the woman comes, Elisha does address himself to her but very curtly (v. 36), saying 'Take up your son'.

The blunt manner in which Elisha treats the woman of Shunem is in glaring contrast to the sympathetic attitude of Elijah towards the widow in Zarephath. There are four other points in which the two stories differ: in the description of the revival ritual, in the relation of the prophets to YHWH, in the representation of the women and in the portrayal of the son.

The Revival Ritual
In the resuscitation scene, the attitude of the two prophets is not the same. Both do pray to YHWH, but only the content of the prayer of Elijah has been reproduced (vv. 20, 21). While it is said of Elisha that he prayed, the content of his prayer remains unknown. On the other hand, Elijah's prayer is extensive, comprising two parts. First he prays for the widow (v. 20), then for the boy (v. 21). Both prayers begin with the invocation:

> YHWH, my God…

Between these two prayers, he stretches himself upon the child. In this manner, Elijah's *words* receive much attention, while his *actions* are described only summarily. In the case of Elisha it is exactly the other way around: this prophet hardly speaks, but his actions are given ample description.[23] In terms of literary composition the two revival scenes are more or less parallel, thus lending more emphasis to the points of contrast between the performances of the two prophets:

---

23. The twice repeated ויגהר 'he bent himself over him' (vv. 34-35) is striking. The Hebrew verb which is used here only occurs further in 1 Kgs 18.42, where it describes Elijah's posture on Mt Carmel when he is pleading for rain. Cf. Robinson, *The Second Book of Kings*, p. 46.

1 Kings 17	2 Kings 4
reproach of the woman (v. 18)	reproach of the woman (v. 28)
prophet to the woman (v. 19)	prophet to the servant (v. 29)
prayer to YHWH (vv. 20-21) (content known)	prayer to YHWH (v. 33c) (content *un*known)
ritual action: stretches himself (v. 21a)	*ritual action:* stands up lays himself down places mouth upon mouth eye upon eye hand upon hand bends himself over the child (v. 34) returns walks back and forth in the house ascends bends himself over the child (v. 35)
	prophet to servant: call the Shunammite
prophet to woman: your son lives (v. 23)	prophet to woman: take up your son (v. 36)

From their first meetings with the women, it is apparent how differently the two prophets behave. Elijah goes purposefully to Zarephath, commissioned by the word of YHWH (1 Kgs 17.8-10). Elisha passes (by accident?) by Shunem one day (2 Kgs 4.8). In story 1 it is Elijah who takes the initiative in contacting the woman: he asks her for water and bread, and insists that the woman provide this for him (1 Kgs 17.11-14). In story 2 it is not the prophet but the woman who takes the initiative (2 Kgs 4.8). She practically forces Elisha to stay with her. It is true that there is as yet no upper room, but she will have it built in due course. She places several pieces of furniture in the room and, in particular, a bed, a piece of furniture which also plays a role in the story of Elijah.[24]

YHWH

The relation of the two prophets to YHWH exhibits great contrast. In story 1 the name of YHWH is heard fourteen times. Elijah is called twice by 'the word of YHWH' (vv. 2, 8) and he 'acts according to the

---

24. In the story about the son of Jezebel, again, a 'bed' is mentioned (2 Kgs 1.4, 6, 16).

word of YHWH' (v. 5). Thrice the name of YHWH is heard from Elijah's mouth (vv. 1, 20, 21) and YHWH listens to him (v. 22). In story 2 the name of YHWH is mentioned but three times, once by the prophet who speaks of his God in a negative sense (2 Kgs 4.27):

> YHWH has hidden it from me
> and has not made it known to me.

The woman uses the name of YHWH when she reminds Elisha of his calling (v. 30). Finally, the reader is informed that Elisha prays to YHWH (v. 33).

The Women

Observing the portrayal of the two women, we notice much similarity, especially in the words they utter. It has already been mentioned that the last words of the widow are practically the same as the first words of the Shunammite. The widow says (1 Kgs 17.24):

> Now I know
> surely, a man of God are you.

The woman of Shunem says (2 Kgs 4.9):

> But see, I know
> surely, a holy man of God is he.[25]

At another point in both of the stories, the woman addresses the prophet with the title 'man of God' (1 Kgs 17.18; 2 Kgs 4.16). Furthermore, in each story there is one scene in which the woman is not at one with the prophet's way of acting. Both women protest and introduce their objection in an identical manner, namely, by calling on the name of YHWH (1 Kgs 17.12; 2 Kgs 4.30):

> חי יהוה, 'by the life of YHWH'.

Besides these correspondences, there are also differences. The woman in story 1 has no husband but has a son. The woman in story 2 has a husband but not (yet) a son. 'Her husband is old', says Gehazi (v. 14). When the prophet promises her a son, no mention is made of the father. When the child becomes ill, the father shoves the responsibility off onto the mother (v. 19). When the child dies the woman does not report this to her husband, nor does she share with him the reason of her trip to Elisha. In the rest of the story, the father plays no role. Both women act uncommonly independently. The widow of Zarephath has

---

25. The Shunammite strengthens her statement by adding 'holy'.

no husband; she is called the 'mistress of the house' (v. 17). The Shu-nammite does have a husband, but he plays an extremely passive role.

The Son
In story 1 the son is hardly in the picture. He is, as it were, hidden behind his mother. Seven times he is referred to by the word בֵּן, 'son', a repeated reminder of his relationship to his mother:

> me and *my* son (v. 12).
> you and *your* son (v. 13).
>> the son of the *woman* (v. 17).
>> *my* son: dying (v. 18).
>>> give me *your* son (v. 19).
>> *her* son: dying (v. 20).
> *your* son: living (v. 23).

Additionally, the boy is indicated as הַיֶּלֶד, 'the child', four times, namely, when Elijah is alone with him in his room and the mother is not involved (vv. 21 [2×], 22, 23).

In story 2 there is initially no son present.[26] The first time that the word 'son' is mentioned is when Gehazi makes Elisha aware of the absence of a son (v. 14). In total, the word בֵּן, 'son', occurs six times in this text:

> no *son* (negative) (v. 14).
>> Elisha speaks: you will embrace a *son* (v. 16).
>>> she bears a *son* (fulfilment of promise) (v. 17).
>>> asked for a *son*? (promise in question) (v. 28).
>> Elisha speaks: take your *son* (v. 36).
> she takes her *son* (positive) (v. 37).

At other points in the story the boy is indicated as הַיֶּלֶד, 'the child', four times (vv. 18, 26, 34 [2×]) or as הַנַּעַר, 'the boy', seven times (vv. 29, 30, 31 [2×], 32, 35 [2×]). What is the course of the illness and death of the boy in the two stories? In the story of Elijah the description is extremely brief (1 Kgs 17.17):

> The son became ill,
> his illness was very severe,
> until there was no breath left in him.

In the story of Elisha the description is thorough and expressive. The child goes out of doors, arrives at the reapers and says to his father (2 Kgs 4.19):

> My head, my head!

26. Neither are the other elements of the resuscitation scene (upper room, bed).

Since this is the only time in which the boy has a line to say, his utterance is undoubtedly of importance. What is the matter with the head of the boy? Has he got sunstroke, as commentators assume? Or is the boy asking about his origin, as van Dijk-Hemmes suggests: 'The boy wants to know who is his "head", his father'.[27] Is there here a suggestion that the man of God could be the father of the boy? In any case, he is the spiritual father: without the man of God there would have been no son. What do the words of the boy have to do with the prophet?

The fact that the boy is unnamed offers the opportunity of diverting the attention from the personal identity of this 'son' to his possible narrative function in the story, namely, as a metaphor for the 'sons of Israel'.[28] In the books of Kings it appears that things have gone amiss with the 'head' of this people[29] with the result that the 'son'—Israel—cannot live. The 'man of God' must revive the 'son'! This is the calling of a prophet.[30]

Elijah comes up to the expectations of his calling: he faces the confrontation with the king (1 Kgs 17.1; 18.18) and with the people (1 Kgs 18.21). In contrast, we do not hear of Elisha addressing the people, nor do we hear of him summoning the king to reconsider his ways. On this issue, Elisha fails. The story depicts the woman as the one who understands what it is all about. She is the one who recalls to him his calling (2 Kgs 4.30):

חי יהוה, 'by the life of YHWH',
I shall not leave you...

27. Van Dijk-Hemmes, 'The Great Woman', p. 226.
28. In story 1 we saw as well that through the son reference is made to the people. Cf. Tamis Hoover Rentería: 'It is necessary to understand that while the stories may reflect actual interactions between particular individuals and a prophet, they cannot be fully understood unless these individuals are seen as generic characters, representatives of sub-groups of people' ('The Elijah/Elisha Stories: A Socio-Cultural Analysis of Prophets and People in Ninth-Century B.C.E. Israel', in Robert B. Coote [ed.], *Elijah and Elisha in Socioliterary Perspective* [Atlanta: Scholars Press, 1992], pp. 75-126 [97]).
29. 'The king does "that which is evil", he threatens and is powerless'. Cf. Aleida G. van Daalen, 'Vertel mij toch al het grote dat Elisa gedaan heeft', *Amsterdamse Cahiers voor Exegese en Bijbelse Theologie* 5 (1984), pp. 118-34 (128).
30. Nonetheless, Elisha does not act. 'We would expect Elisha to challenge verbally the actions of the kings and/or the people': Bergen, 'Prophetic Alternative', p. 135.

Conclusion

The most striking correspondence between the two stories is the reviving of the son. It is possible to take the resuscitation scene as a reference to the calling of the prophet as God's man 'to breathe new life into God's child, Israel, who was fast becoming spiritually lifeless'.[31]

The comparison of the two stories shows that Elisha has difficulties with his role as 'man of God' and as 'successor to Elijah'. Although initially this story sets the stage so that Elisha could act as Elijah did, Elisha is not presented as doing so, instead remaining passive. When he hears that the son has died, he does not come himself but sends his servant. Concerning Elijah in story 1, his relationship to his divine Commissioner is clear: the 'word of YHWH' is in his mouth. As for Elisha, the matter is turbid: he can only report that YHWH has held the matter hidden from him and has not made it known to him (2 Kgs 4.27). Thanks to the woman's persistence, Elisha does eventually also revive the son. This act is important in the continuation of the tales of Elisha: the reviving of the son is cited in a following story as proof of 'all the great things' which Elisha had done (2 Kgs 8.4). Because the man of God had revived the 'son', the woman and her son are given back their house and field (2 Kgs 8.4-6).[32]

It is remarkable that Elisha himself seems to attach little importance to the fact that the son is no longer dead but *alive*. This becomes particularly apparent in a comparison of the closing scenes of the two stories. Elijah realizes that a miracle has taken place: 'See, your son *lives*'. Elisha merely gives an order: 'Take up your son'. The woman in the first story reacts with an exuberant testimony in which the trustworthiness of the 'word of YHWH' assumes a central place (1 Kgs 17.24). The woman in the second story is silent. She kneels in deep adoration for the *prophet* and performs his command: she takes up her son and leaves (2 Kgs 4.37).

In the following stories as well, a great difference in the concern of

31. Robinson, *The First Book of Kings*, p. 203. Robinson's remark concerns only the prophet Elijah but it is undoubtedly also true for Elisha.

32. Could one here assume a metaphoric relation between this 'son' and the 'sons of Israel' as well? In such a case, the 'return to house and land' could refer to the exodus of the 'sons of Israel', where similarly a seven-year famine was the cause for the departure from one's own land (cf. 2 Kgs 8.1-3). In Exodus as well, the 'death–life' theme is a central element. Cf. Jopie Siebert-Hommes, *Let the Daughters Live! The Literary Architecture of Exodus 1–2 as a Key for Interpretation* (Leiden: E.J. Brill, 1998), pp. 94-101.

the prophets comes to light. Elijah's message is aimed at revealing to the people and the king that there is a *God in Israel* (cf. 2 Kgs 1.3). Elisha, however, does his utmost to make known that there is a *prophet in Israel* (2 Kgs 5.8). 'Elisha has no message', observes Wesley J. Bergen with surprise.[33]

In the discrepancy sketched above between Elisha as prophet and the manner in which he practices this prophetic calling, both of the women have a special function. Just as the prophets are each other's successors, so are the women, viewed as a literary device. The first woman *ends:* 'I know, you are a man of God' (1 Kgs 17.24). The second woman *begins:* 'I know, he is a holy man of God' (2 Kgs 4.9).

The second woman, however, is then confronted with a prophet who apparently has difficulties with his calling. The actions of this woman are directed at reminding him of his calling. She first lays her son on the bed of the man of God (in the first story, it was the prophet who did that himself), then she hastens to him and speaks the very words with which Elisha himself once became the successor of Elijah. These words cause the prophet to rise and, *following* the woman (2 Kgs 4.30), to show himself to be the true successor of Elijah.

Van Dijk-Hemmes too recognizes the role of the Shunammite as crucial in the second story. 'The memory of this woman deserves to be kept alive', she declares; and she proposes to pay her the homage that the biblical text withheld from her: the woman can be named. And what name is more appropriate than the adjective with which she is introduced?[34] With Fokkelien, let us call the woman *Gᵉdôlāh*, the 'Great One'.

---

33. Bergen, 'Prophetic Alternative', p. 135. Bergen gives an extensive treatment of the sociological-cultural context of the Elijah/Elisha stories and from that context he gives some reasons for this lack of message (p. 136).

34. אשה גדולה, 'a great woman' (2 Kgs 4.8). See van Dijk-Hemmes, 'The Great Woman', p. 230.

indirect dialogue—Elisha speaks to the woman almost exclusively
through Gehazi, his servant—likewise enhances Elisha's power; and
the miracle he performs is also what we expect of a 'man of God'.

Yet there are disjunctions, both within the story itself and between
this story and the parallel Elijah narrative in 1 Kings 17, which invite
the reader to question the surface perspective. One finds upon a closer
reading that the roles, and indeed the power, of Elisha and the
Shunammite woman are surprisingly reversed. The first clue we have
to this reversal is the characterization of the woman. She is called an
'iššâ gᵉdôlâ (lit. 'great woman') in v. 8, an ambiguous term that apparently describes her as a woman of means—she builds the man of God
a chamber—but also, given her further actions and words, comes to
describe her independence and status in her own right. For example,
the husband is defined only in relation to the woman in this story.
While she receives a title, he is known only as 'her husband'. This
highly unusual state of affairs is reflected in their relationship as well.
The Shunammite woman stands out as the active partner, while her
husband merely goes along with her wishes. It is she who invites the
man of God to eat bread when he passes, and she proposes adding a
room to their house for Elisha to stay in when he comes. The only
time the husband takes action is when he questions the woman as she
sets out to find the man of God after her son dies (v. 23). Even then, in
response to his question about why she should go at such an unusual
time, the woman simply evades answering him and goes on her way.

The contrasted activity and passivity are not only present in her
marriage, however, but are characteristic of the relations between the
woman and Elisha as well. Elisha's actions are always in response to
the woman's initiative. For instance, it is because she has provided a
place for him to stay that the man of God desires to give the woman a
gift. And when her son dies, he finds out about it and returns to perform the miracle only because the woman has come and asked him to
do so. In addition, there is the same sort of contrast between the characters of Elisha and Elijah in the parallel narrative in which Elijah
raises a widow's son from the dead. At the beginning of the 2 Kings 4
narrative, Elisha does not say anything; he merely comes and stays
whenever he passes through. In the 1 Kings 17 story, on the other
hand, Elijah initiates all the action. He asks for food and drink and
promises continued sustenance until the coming of the rain. Furthermore, when the widow's son in the 1 Kings 17 narrative becomes sick
and the widow complains, Elijah, in a quick sequence of actions, acts
to remedy the situation. When the son of the woman of Shunem dies,
however, Elisha is not even present. But even when she finally does

reach him, he sends his servant rather than going himself. It is only through the woman's continued persistence that he comes at all— which is fortunate, since Gehazi is unsuccessful. Thus, Elisha's character as a man of God also suffers in comparison with the other great man of God, Elijah.

In addition to the contrasting initiative of the woman and passivity of Elisha, there are other indications that neither of the characters is what they at first seemed. As mentioned before, throughout the first scene in which the woman invites and prepares, she is portrayed as active, in charge, independent. The second scene opens, however, with the first action being that of Elisha. In response to all the care given to him, the prophet decides to reward the woman. Thus, he asks his servant, Gehazi, to call the Shunammite woman. When she appears, he asks Gehazi to offer some reward for the woman's hospitality.

Two things are notable about this exchange. First, Elisha's offer is to use his influence with the king or commander of the army on her behalf, an offer that highlights their difference in status. Second, throughout their interchange, Elisha does not speak directly to her— in fact there are only two places where he uses direct speech: when announcing the coming birth of her son (v. 16), and, after raising her son from the dead, when telling her to lift up her son (v. 36). Even in these interchanges, however, he uses Gehazi as a go-between. The actual wording of the summons to the woman plays on power differences. The syntax (*qr' l*... or *qr' 'l*...) is often used in summoning servants.[1] The term he uses for the woman is also politically charged: by calling her 'this Shunammite' (vv. 12, 36), Elisha not only avoids naming her (a classic status differentiation tactic), but he may in fact be indicating a kind of contempt for her status.[2] In Elisha's speech the *'iššâ gᵉdôlâ* of Shunem is reduced simply to 'this Shunammite'.

Elisha is thus pictured preserving the difference in status he enjoys as the man of God over against this woman of Shunem.[3] Yet the boundaries Elisha has set are broken by the woman almost immediately. Although Elisha's questions are addressed to her through Gehazi, the Shunammite woman answers Elisha directly. Moreover,

1. See, for example, Gen. 20.8; Num. 22.5, 21; 2 Sam. 1.17; Job 19.16.
2. See GKC §136; BDB, p. 260.
3. So also, B.O. Long, 'A Figure at the Gate: Readers, Reading, and Biblical Theologians', in G.M. Tucker *et al.* (eds.), *Canon, Theology and Old Testament Interpretation* (Philadelphia: Fortress Press, 1988), pp. 169-70. There are several similarities in argument between this article and my own reading, with one of the major differences being my focus on feminist issues in interpretation.

her answer to the offer is one that asserts her own status in the community and her independence. The words 'I dwell among my own
people' (v. 13) say, in effect, 'No thanks, I do fine on my own. My people will provide if I have need.' The woman thus retains equal footing
with the man of God in the first verbal exchange of this narrative.

However, Elisha is not satisfied with the woman's answer and asks
Gehazi what can be done for her. His answer reveals, for the first time
in this story, that she is childless. Moreover, the cause of her childlessness is implied to be her husband's age rather than her barrenness.
Notice that the woman's response to the pronouncement (to the 'gift'
that Elisha promises to her) is once again resistance. The words themselves, however, are ambiguous: 'No, my lord, O man of God; do not
lie to your maidservant'. The particular construction used here—*lō'*
occurring twice, followed first by an address to someone else, and
second by a verb—occurs only two other times in the OT, both of
which are rape contexts.[4] Thus, the words may be a refusal of a gift
she has not requested, and may not desire; they may imply distrust of
the man of God or of his motives. In either case, the man of God's
power is questioned. Moreover, the use of the word 'lie' acts to fore-
shadow the future death of the child. Nevertheless, the man of God's
words come true—she bears a son.

The scene where Elisha promises the child to the woman follows
the pattern of the so-called 'annunciation type-scene' discussed by
Alter.[5] J.G. Williams has refined the scene into two types: the contest
of the barren wife and the promise to the barren wife. Our story falls
in the latter category, which according to Williams has five common
elements: (1) the wife is barren; (2) a messenger from God appears to
the woman; (3) the messenger promises a son; (4) the event is con-
firmed in spite of human doubt, and (5) the promised son is born and
given a significant name.[6]

2 Kings 4, however, does not completely fit the pattern. First, as
noted before, the woman is described neither as barren nor as desiring
a child. Secondly, while Elisha holds the title 'man of God', God is
conspicuously absent in the interchange between him and the Shunammite woman. In each of the other cases, the child to be born has

---

4.   Judg. 19.23 and 2 Sam. 13.12.

5.   R. Alter, 'How Convention Helps us Read: The Case of the Bible's Annunciation Type-Scene', *Prooftexts* 3 (1983), pp. 115-30. See especially pp. 125-26 for
Alter's treatment of this story, which is similar to my own.

6.   J.G. Williams, *Women Recounted: Narrative Thinking and the God of Israel*
(Sheffield: Almond Press, 1982), pp. 48-55.

great significance for Israel, and it is by God's command that the child is promised. Here, in contrast, the child serves merely as a foil for the great miracle Elisha will perform. Moreover, the child is *Elisha's* gift to the woman. Neither God nor the woman is consulted in the matter. The absence of God also raises an issue that will become important later—that of responsibility. Who is responsible for the life of this child? God? The woman? It would seem that the only party to the decision is Elisha. The fourth element is also anomalous in this story. As mentioned before, the woman does more than doubt: she actually resists the man of God's pronouncement. Finally, the last element does not appear at all—the child is not given a significant name because he himself is not significant. An added anomaly is the husband's absence from the scene. Even in Judges 13, the other parallel annunciation scene where the wife dominates,[7] the husband involves himself to some degree. The contrast not only implies that Elisha's gift is intended for the woman alone, thereby emphasizing her central place in the story, but it also raises the question of the parentage of the child.[8]

Thus the scene depicted in vv. 11-16 is recognizable as a parody of the annunciation type-scene. In it, Elisha diminishes the woman's status by taking away her ability to decide what she does and does not want. Yet Elisha does not appear to be in charge of the exchange either. Once again, he acts not on his own initiative, but on the advice of his servant. On the other hand, the Shunammite's status is elevated as opposed to her husband. The gift is given to her alone, thus reinforcing her independence and dominance vis-à-vis her husband.

With the narrator's description of the boy's birth and growth in vv. 17 and 18, the scene is set for the miracle story—the climax of the narrative. The action begins in v. 19, when the child becomes sick in the field, is sent home by his father, and dies in his mother's lap. It is notable here that the husband does not assume responsibility for the child—in one of only two speeches by the Shunammite woman's hus-

---

7. Most recent commentators agree that Manoah's wife is the focal point of the annunciation scene in Judg. 13, whereas Manoah himself is left out of the main action and is unaware of what is really taking place (see Williams, *Women Recounted*, p. 54; Alter, 'Convention', pp. 123-24; J.C. Exum, 'Promise and Fulfillment: Narrative Art in Judges 13', *JBL* 99 [1980], pp. 43-59).

8. L.R. Klein has already raised such a question with regard to the Samson birth narrative (*The Triumph of Irony in the Book of Judges* [JSOTSup, 68; Sheffield: JSOT Press, 1989], p. 114). The question looms even larger in a story where the husband is conspicuous by his absence.

band in this story, he instructs a servant to take the child home to his mother.[9]

Upon the child's death, the mother acts quickly, repeating the very actions in v. 21 (carrying him to the man of God's room, laying him on the bed, and shutting the door) that the man of God, Elijah, performed in the parallel story (1 Kgs 17.19). The next few verses portray the woman acting quickly and decisively to do what she can for her son. After asking her husband to send for one of the servants, and brushing aside his questions with a brusque 'It is well' (v. 23),[10] she saddles the donkey and directs the servant to ride with all speed to Elisha. The Shunammite dominates this scene as she does the first, both in relation to the other characters and in the quickness and decisiveness of her activity. This will contrast with Elisha's behavior in the next scene.

The next scene opens in v. 25 with the approach of the woman to the man of God at Mt Carmel. When Elisha notices her approach from some distance, he sends Gehazi to ask her if everything is well (v. 26). By this act, he still preserves the distance between himself and the woman; Gehazi remains the go-between, at least from Elisha's end. Once again, however, the Shunammite woman refuses to acknowledge the distance Elisha attempts to place between them, this time by refusing to tell Gehazi what is wrong. Her response to the servant echoes her response to her husband: 'It is well'.[11] Neither her husband nor Gehazi needs to know what has happened—her words are reserved for Elisha alone. Hence, she goes straight to the man of God. This time, however, when Gehazi attempts to thrust her away, Elisha responds by telling him to leave her alone.

In this scene the woman's status is elevated at the expense of that of Elisha in several ways. First, although the man of God perceives her

9. The husband's lack of involvement once again raises the question not only of responsibility for the child but also of the child's parentage. Who *is* the father of this child? (See also v. 14, where it is implied that he is too old to become a father.)

10. The husband's question to the woman, 'Why are you going to him when it is neither new moon nor Sabbath', implies that he does not connect the woman's trip with the sickness of the child. His lack of awareness is perhaps a further indication of his lack of responsibility for this child.

11. In a text where the politics of power play such a major role, the fact that the woman uses the same words to her husband that she uses to Gehazi places the husband on the level of Gehazi in the story. Just as Gehazi is given orders by Elisha, so the husband is given orders by his wife (v. 22). Additionally, her very words, 'it is well', mislead them both as to the true nature of her trip. Once again the implication is that the responsibility for this child is Elisha's.

anguish, he has no idea what the cause is. In fact, YHWH has hidden it from him (v. 27). Thus, the man of God, the one who *should* know, must wait for the woman to enlighten him. Her words of accusation ('Didn't I say to you, "Don't deceive me?!"') bear this out. The woman's question also reminds the man of God that she did not request a child and alludes to her resistance when the promise was given (v. 16). The child is, by implication, Elisha's responsibility.

Rather than answering her or taking action himself, however, Elisha tells Gehazi to hurry with his staff to heal the child, thus attempting to evade the responsibility of which the Shunammite woman reminded him. Yet he is not to be let off so easily. The woman insists that she will not return without the man of God, and he finally goes with her. Once again the initiative is the woman's, and this time Elisha is the reluctant follower. The roles are once again reversed—no longer is the woman in awe of the man of God. The reader is likewise freed of this attitude: we applaud the woman's assertiveness, especially when we find out in the next verse (v. 31) that Elisha's staff has not worked. Just as Elisha's evasion of responsibility has not worked, so his power has not worked. He must himself be present.

When Elisha does arrive, his power is nearly inadequate: the boy only recovers by stages between which Elisha must get up and walk about. Is it implied that he is at first not quite powerful enough to cure the child? An affirmative answer is strengthened by the woman's original response to the promise of a child in v. 16. Perhaps the gift he offered her was one he had no right to offer except when instructed by YHWH. In this case, the reference to YHWH's hiding knowledge from Elisha (and Elisha's preliminary failure as well) could be YHWH's judgment on the prophet's hubris, which the woman sensed in some way when she resisted the gift.

A closer reading of 2 Kgs 4.8-37 reveals that the story as a whole presents a subtle critique of the man of God and his wonder-working, evidenced by the surprising power and role reversals between the woman of Shunem and the man of God. Where the ostensible power throughout the story is in the hands of Elisha, the real power rests with the woman. It is she who is the main actor in the story, while Elisha is primarily the reactor. It is she who breaks through the boundaries Elisha continually tries to set, thus undercutting his rank and authority. It is she who, apart from the miracle itself, completes the actions necessary to have the child resuscitated. Finally, it is she who reminds Elisha of his responsibility and, when he tries to avoid it, forces him to be accountable.

Yet this is not the final word in the narrative. If the roles and power are reversed in the interior of the story itself, they are nevertheless restored at the end. The narrative concludes with YHWH allowing Elisha to cure the child and the Shunammite woman bowing in gratitude at Elisha's feet.[12] Moreover, in the sequel in 2 Kings 8, the story of her son's revival is interpreted as evidence of the wonder-working power of Elisha. Thus, while a woman may have a primary, even powerful role in the narrative, she is not allowed to maintain such a role. Although the woman is elevated for a while, the patriarchal perspective wins out in the end. Thus, in this text there is a tension between a woman-elevating or gynocentric point of view and a patriarchal or androcentric point of view.

In the patriarchal world that the Bible represents, even when gender roles and power are reversed, they cannot remain reversed. The patriarchal perspective will and must inevitably return and predominate. This is necessary because women are seen, to quote Toril Moi, 'as occupying a marginal position within the symbolic order' in a patriarchal system. Furthermore, patriarchy must keep women marginalized to survive.[13] It is thus dangerous for a woman to remain in a position of strength. Therefore the final scene, in which the roles once again revert to 'normal', is necessary.

This patriarchal perspective intrudes in several other aspects of the story as well. The first clue to the patriarchal perspective occurs in the first scene. Although the woman is described as an *'iššâ gᵉdôlâ*, she is never given a name. Namelessness is one symbolic political tactic by which patriarchy asserts its dominance over women. The act of naming implicitly confers status and power. By not giving the woman of Shunem a name, the political and patriarchal scales are weighted in favour of the male characters who are given names—Elisha, the man of God, and even his servant, Gehazi.

A second way in which the patriarchal perspective predominates is in the type of gift given to the woman. Anyone viewing this from a patriarchal perspective would never suspect that a childless woman's first wish might not be for a child. This is borne out by the many articles and commentaries written by men on this story. No one thinks to ask whether a child is really the woman of Shunem's greatest

---

12. Note, however, that there is no final verbal interchange between Elisha and the woman of Shunem. While the act of bowing is itself appropriate, one wonders whether some irony is intended—although the woman pays proper homage, does her silence indicate implicit mocking of this man of God?

13. T. Moi, *Sexual/Textual Politics: Feminist Literary Theory* (London: Routledge, 1985), p. 167.

desire.[14] What does this say about the ways in which hidden patriarchy is prevalent even today? However, in the story itself patriarchal ideology is much more evident. As Esther Fuchs says of the annunciation type-scene in general, it 'drives home the...message that woman has no control at all over her reproductive potential'.[15] Fuchs' statement rings true for this story in particular: it is very clear that Elisha is the one who controls the woman's child-bearing.

Yet another indication of the patriarchal perspective is the way in which the Shunammite woman's actions are portrayed as the typical ideal mother: she is protective of her child and relentlessly devoted to him.[16] When the child becomes sick and dies, she fights for the restoration of his life. This too follows the patriarchal political agenda. As Fuchs says, 'to acknowledge woman's disinterest in children would undermine one of the major premises of patriarchal thought: that woman always desires to be a mother'.[17]

Finally, despite the central role the Shunammite plays in this story, 'the literary frame of the unit', to use Fuchs' words, 'opening and concluding with information regarding male characters attests to the patriarchal ideology underlying them'.[18] Thus, although the man of God's power and status are subverted by the woman of Shunem, the woman's power and status are in turn subverted by the patriarchal perspective, particularly in the closing scene, where she reverts to the patriarchally appropriate role of admiring subject.

But this negative reading is not the final word either. Danna Nolan Fewell writes, 'we cannot naively accept positive feminist texts as unmediated words of liberation; neither can we reject negative patriarchal texts as unredeemable words of subjugation'.[19] I would argue

---

14. Gressmann's comments are typical when he says that the birth announcement 'spricht das Sehnen ihres Herzens aus, den Wunsch, den sie dem Propheten selbst aus Bescheidenheit und Scheu verschwiegen hat' (*Die Schriften des Alten Testaments* [Göttingen: Vandenhoeck & Ruprecht, 2nd edn, 1921], p. 293). Even many scholars who are not as blatant imply, by their translation of the words 'do not lie' in v. 16 as 'do not raise false hopes', that a child is the woman's greatest desire (see, for example, Alter, 'Convention', p. 125; R. Kilian, 'Die Totenerweckungen Elias und Elisas—Eine Motivwanderung?', *BZ* 10 [1966], p. 46).

15. E. Fuchs, 'The Literary Characterization of Mothers and Sexual Politics in the Hebrew Bible', in A. Yarbro Collins (ed.), *Feminist Perspectives on Biblical Scholarship* (Chico, CA: Scholars Press, 1985), p. 129.

16. Fuchs, 'Literary Characterization', p. 133.

17. Fuchs, 'Literary Characterization', p. 133.

18. Fuchs, 'Literary Characterization', p. 136.

19. D.N. Fewell, 'Feminist Reading of the Hebrew Bible: Affirmation, Resistance and Transformation', *JSOT* 39 (1987), p. 77-87 (82).

that in this text we find a unique blend of the two perspectives—neither canceling the other out. Thus, Fewell's words are well taken. The fact that the patriarchal gender roles are restored at the end does not negate the fact that a woman is elevated at the expense of the man of God. I would suggest further that it is no accident that a woman, a representative of those who are marginalized in society, does the subverting. The subversion is all the more effective because it is one whose gender would normally marginalize her who challenges the structure of sacred authority. If the patriarchal or androcentric view wins out in the end, there is nevertheless a gynocentric emphasis that cannot be completely hidden.

SELF-RESPONSE TO 'SUBVERTING A MAN OF GOD, ELEVATING A WOMAN: ROLE AND POWER REVERSALS IN 2 KINGS 4'

Mary E. Shields

As I look back on this article, I remain pleased with the close reading I did, and the ways in which I highlighted some of the gender and power dynamics at work in the story of the great woman of Shunem. This article was my first foray into feminist biblical interpretation. At times the article betrays its age (the patriarchal nature of biblical texts has since become a commonplace), or over-zealous reading (for example, my initial statements overstate the case a bit: within patriarchal societies women *do* have some power, but it is usually not in the public sphere, and there are several cases where women step outside the patriarchal power structures just as the great woman of Shunem does; for instance, Tamar in Gen. 38, and Deborah in Judg. 4). Yet on balance I stand by my article as an articulate close reading of the story in 2 Kgs 4.8-37, which went beyond other treatments to that date.

In addition to those named above, there are two other modifications which I would make were I writing this article today. First, there is an error in my account of the language used by the woman in response to Elisha's 'gift' of a child (v. 16). Instead of beginning with *lô'* the construction used both here and in two rape scenes begins with *'al*. Second, if I were writing today on this text, I would probably not raise the possibility of the woman not wanting a child; in retrospect this idea seems anachronistic. However, I wish to continue to emphasize my related argument that the woman has a strongly negative reaction to Elisha's pronouncement that she would have a child.

In the remainder of my response I will engage in dialogue with an excellent recent article on 2 Kgs 4.8-37 written by S. Brent Plate and Edna M. Rodríguez Mangual.[1] Viewing this text through the lens of Hélène Cixous' discussion of economies of giving, Plate and Rodríguez Mangual have developed my reading in significant ways.

---

1. S. Brent Plate, and E.M. Rodríguez Mangual, 'The Gift that Stops Giving: Hélène Cixous's "Gift" and the Shunammite Woman', *BibInt* 7.2 (1999), pp. 113-32.

According to Cixous' model as the authors present it, by giving the man of God a place to stay whenever he passes through, the great woman of Shunem gives a gift within the feminine 'Realm of the Gift' because she has no expectation or desire for reciprocity. Elisha, on the other hand, uncomfortable with this Realm, seeks to place the situation back on an even-exchange footing, thereby attempting to return to the masculine 'Realm of the Proper' in which 'what is given is immediately "taken up" into a circuit of exchange whereby the gift must be paid back'.[2]

Through a careful juxtaposition of Cixous' work with a close reading of the biblical text, Plate and Rodríguez Mangual make a convincing argument regarding the power dynamics of the gifts in the story. Building on my work, they show how the exchanges in this story, verbal and otherwise, illustrate ways in which Elisha seeks not only to restore equilibrium after receiving the special room by reciprocating the gift (return to the Realm of the Proper), but actually to get 'one up' on the woman, thereby coming out as master.[3] In addition, they address an issue already discussed above: the resistance of the woman to Elisha's 'gift' of a child. They read this resistance partially as a resistance to moving from the Realm of the Gift to the Realm of the Proper.

Using as a springboard my allusion to the rape language in the scene where Elisha announces the coming of a child despite the woman's protestations, they go a step further and read the entire scene as a rape scene. While I think the authors overstate the case when they call this scene a rape 'type-scene',[4] their carefully crafted reading nonetheless is particularly persuasive in dealing with power dynamics at work in the story.[5] Of particular note are: (a) the specific links they make between this scene and the rape scene in 2 Samuel 13;[6] (b) the central place of the bed as the site of both types of exchange (Realm of the Gift and Realm of the Proper);[7] and (c) their argumentation for the woman's conception being a forced conception.[8] Finally, their conclusion that 'Elisha went too far with his giving—the unavoidable result of the masculine economy: never know-

---

2.   Plate and Rodríguez Mangual, 'The Gift', p. 117.
3.   'The Gift', pp. 120-22.
4.   'The Gift', p 126; basing the designation 'type-scene' on two examples alone is slim in my view.
5.   Cf. 'The Gift', pp. 127-128.
6.   'The Gift', p. 127.
7.   'The Gift', p. 127.
8.   'The Gift', pp. 127-28.

ing when to stop, by appropriating 'the great woman (and particularly her body) in his desire to play the annunciation scene and be
the holy messenger from God',[9] well illustrates the power dynamic at
work in Elisha's actions toward the woman of Shunem. Moreover,
these arguments not only reinforce my reading of the role reversals
and power dynamics in the story, but extend it substantially.

The one point at which I think their article is on shaky ground,
however, is their conclusion. I think they make a good case for reading Elisha's restoration of life to the young boy in the final section of
the story as being within the Realm of the Gift, since it is a gift of 'life
without taking anything back'.[10] They see Elisha's actions as illus-
trating this principle:

> The prophet's body becomes like that of a pregnant woman in that he
> doubles his body by mimetically stretching on top of the boy's body.
> Giving is a doubling. It is recognition, but a recognition that must give
> without return. At this moment, thanks to the woman that brought him
> into this situation, the prophet enters into the Realm of the Gift. He
> gives, but he gives a gift which will not, cannot, enter the cycle of proper
> exchange.[11]

While I agree with this reading, I do not agree with their argument
that Elisha's actions result in his transformation, 'where he gives…a
life that is not bound up with a circuit of exchange'.[12] On the contrary, I do see Elisha receiving something in exchange for giving life
to the boy. In the sequel in 2 Kings 8, it is clear that his status and
power within the political domain have been enhanced by this miracle.

2 Kings 8.1-7 begins with Elisha sending the woman and her son
to another country to escape a famine which he has predicted. The
remaining verses focus on her return at the end of the famine. As the
woman comes to the king to ask for the return of her land, Gehazi is
coincidentally telling the king about Elisha's great miracle of raising a
boy from the dead. Seeing the woman and her son, Gehazi uses them
to prove the veracity of his story. Once again, I agree with Plate's and
Rodríguez Mangual's reading, that Elisha continues his 'mothering'
role by warning the Shunammite woman to leave the country before a
famine (2 Kgs 8.1). However, Elisha himself has benefited within the
Realm of the Proper from his deed; the fact that the woman and her

9.   'The Gift', p. 128.
10. 'The Gift', p. 120
11. 'The Gift', p. 131.
12. 'The Gift', p. 131.

son are living testimonies to his power enhances Elisha's prestige. That Elisha, through Gehazi in this instance, trades on this story with those with political power shows clearly that the gift of life is now 'bound up within a circuit of exchange',[13] that is, that he has been successful in transferring it from the Realm of the Gift to the Realm of the Proper.

Moreover, in v. 6 it is implied that this story is the reason the king restores the woman of Shunem's land—it is not because of her own status as great woman (*'iššâ gᵉdôlāh*), but rather, because of Elisha's role as miracle worker. Thus, the gift of life has returned to Elisha as status and power, and the masculine economy is restored. Even further, what Elisha (via Gehazi) first offers in exchange for the gift of the room and the bed in 2 Kgs 4.8-37, that is, speaking to the king on the woman's behalf (v. 13), he eventually accomplishes in 2 Kgs 8.1-7: Gehazi functions successfully as the go-between this time (contrast this portion of the story with the scene in 2 Kgs 4.11-16 where Elisha tries unsuccessfully to use Gehazi to maintain distance [differentials in power and status?] between himself and the woman). Finally, Elisha's power, albeit indirectly, accomplishes the woman's restoration of her land. The story itself has become a token of exchange in the political (masculine) realm.

As I argue in my own article on 2 Kgs 4.8-37, the patriarchal structures reign in the end. Thus, while I find Plate's and Rodríguez Mangual's reading of the latter portion of the 2 Kgs 4.8-37 provocative and helpful in many ways, I cannot agree that Elisha's actions stay within the Realm of the Gift. Rather, as with most patriarchal texts, the Realm of the Proper, to use Cixous' terminology, has the last word. That word, however, is not the only word. Both of our articles highlight ways in which the stories of the great woman of Shunem in 2 Kings 4 and 8 unmask some of the problems of patriarchal power.

---

13. 'The Gift', p. 131.

CANNIBAL MOTHERS AND ME:
A MOTHER'S READING OF 2 KINGS 6.24–7.20

Laurel Lanner

2 Kings 6.24–7.20 first came to my attention after I had idly turned to an article by Stuart Lasine.[1] Cannibals in the Bible! I put the article aside and immediately looked for the passage. How was it that I had never heard of this? Jephthah's daughter and the Levite's concubine had filtered through thanks to feminist scholarship, but no cannibals had made it. Perhaps the cannibal mothers were just too terrible for rehabilitation by even the hardiest of feminists. Contrary to what I had anticipated I was not shocked by the cannibal mothers, but I was shocked and puzzled by the passage as a whole. I then turned back to the article. The readings have sat at the back of my mind, disturbing me for several years.

Stanley Fish has called literature a 'kinetic art'.[2] Certainly the experience of reading is a process of ranging back and forth, assessing and reassessing. I will present my reading of this text as it happened. I will first present my reading as an 'average reader' as opposed to the 'critical reader'. The average reader, writes Fowler, is informed by his/her 'beliefs, presuppositions and religious community'.[3] Of course, critical readers are informed by exactly the same things. However, my initial reading is my personal response before reading any critical commentary or essay. I will then put on a critical reader's hat and will interact with the readings of others, particularly those of Lasine. Finally, I will discuss this text in the context of 'my place'.

My reading of this passage, while using the language of reader-response criticism, is not an attempt to locate an implied reader. It is

1.   Stuart Lasine, 'Jehoram and the Cannibal Mothers', *JSOT* 50 (1991), pp. 27-53.
2.   As quoted in Robert M. Fowler, "Who is 'The "Reader" in Reader Response Criticism?', *Semeia* 31 (1985), pp. 5-26 (19).
3.   Robert M. Fowler, 'Reader-Response Criticism: Figuring Mark's Reader', in J.C. Anderson and S.D. Moore (eds.), *Mark and Method: New Approaches in Biblical Studies* (Minneapolis: Fortress Press, 1992), pp. 50-83.

the reading of an actual reader—me. It is informed by my status as a Pakeha[4] mother of three children, who has known neither war nor extreme hunger. I come from a culture that, at least in recent centuries, finds cannibalism abhorrent. I come from a society that still acknowledges a nominal monarchy which for most subjects is totally inaccessible. I come from a society where the weight of power in both church and state still lies with white males. I have been reliant upon the state for an income for most of my adult life.

An Initial Reading

In 2 Kgs 6.24-26, a severe famine is established as a result of the siege of Samaria. The unnamed king of Israel is wandering around the city. He is accessible and a woman approaches him for help. I assume she wants food; the king appears to assume this also. He initially tells her to apply to the Lord, but then he asks her what her problem is. As a king he is shaping up well. Although obviously he is under great stress, he is prepared to talk to a woman he meets in the street. She explains that the deal she had with another woman to cook their respective sons, on successive days, has fallen through. I cannot begin to imagine this level of hunger. How desperate they must be! I think of my son and daughters and cannot envisage the moment that I could kill them for my own needs. I would rather die. But I recall the anecdotal evidence I have read of cannibalism in the Ukraine during collectivization and during the Siege of Leningrad.[5] I realise that I cannot make the assumption that I would rather die. Perhaps these women may have different cultural attitudes to my own. I have heard an Australian settler account of aboriginal Australians eating their children in times of drought in the belief they would be born again.[6] There is no evidence in the Hebrew Bible of such a belief. Even so, bearing and birthing a child has never been so effortless and without risk that a mother could give up a child knowing she could easily

---

4. A New Zealander of European extraction.

5. These stories are virtually impossible to validate, but the 'rumours' are so persistent that the likelihood of there being some base in reality would seem reasonable. Examples can be found in Harrison E. Salisbury, *The Siege of Leningrad* (London: Secker & Warburg, 1969), pp. 452-53, 474-76, 478-81, and Robert Conquest, *The Harvest of Sorrow: Soviet Collectivization and the Terror-Famine* (London: Hutchinson, 1986), pp. 257-58, 326.

6. This settler account which may or may not report the view of the aboriginal group themselves can be found in Mary Durack, *Kings in Grass Castles* (London: Constable, 1959), p. 70.

repeat the experience. There is also the possibility that it was considered reasonable that children who were sick or close to death, would be killed in mercy. Perhaps the children were already dead; the text does not actually say that they were killed. However, if the children had already died of hunger would the reneging mother have made the effort to hide her son's corpse?

I reconsider the nature of the woman's complaint. She is complaining of the injustice that the other woman has hidden her son. The poor woman! Not only has she been brought to the point that she would eat her son, but now her decision has been brought into question by the other woman reneging on the deal. Perhaps she too ought to have waited another day. In her confusion—hunger reduces mental functioning—and desperate state she seeks some sort of reassurance. So what is the king's response? He tears his clothes. (I note that he is wearing hidden sackcloth—peculiar, I think.) He then says something that seems completely irrelevant. What may God do to him? Eat him? Bring him low? Hide him? And why remove Elisha's head? He sends someone off to remove Elisha's head and then doesn't follow through with it. Another decision reneged on. At this point I return to the king's response to the woman. He completely ignores her. She has just told him of an act that would seem to be every mother's horror. She has eaten her own child and he cannot respond to her. Perhaps that is understandable. I would have difficulty finding words. But what is the meaning of his statement? I return to v. 33: 'This trouble is from the Lord', says the king to Elisha. It is? What kind of God can this be?

At this point I need to become an informed or expert reader. I begin to interact with the article and commentaries. Perhaps they will explain it so that I feel comfortable again.

Being a Little Critical

First, I read either side of the passage to gain some context. The text does not fit comfortably with what precedes it. The context would suggest that it is a story slotted in, perhaps to illustrate Elisha's successful prophetic abilities.[7] However, there are some points to be noted. Elisha is 'the man of God' (5.8). He has performed previous miracles, including raising a child from the dead (4.32-37), and feeding the hungry (4.42-44). He does not like to be abused and his curse results in the mauling of 42 boys by bears (2.23-25). The king in

7. Burke O. Long, *2 Kings* (FOTL, 10; Grand Rapids: Eerdmans, 1991), p. 91.

this passage is not named, but is presumed to be Jehoram.[8] Jehoram is an idolater for whom Elisha has no respect (3.13-14), although he helps him out of a tight spot. In ch. 7 Elisha prophesies that food will be available the next day, and sure enough, through the agency of four lepers his prophecy is fulfilled. My uneasiness grows. The cannibal mothers appear to be in the midst of plenty.

I begin to read the passage again, this time in conversation with other 'expert' readers. I will be a resisting reader, although it remains to be seen exactly what or whom I will be resisting.

So how have others read the cannibal mothers? John Gray manages to avoid mentioning them at all. His only comment, on 8.28-29, is that cannibalism was a common thing in antiquity in times of famine and siege. The women and their problem are unmentioned. He does note that the sackcloth of the king symbolizes his sympathy with the suffering people. He suggests the king's response concerning Elisha is because he feared riots and sought Elisha as a scapegoat.[9] Has this reader seen the woman standing there?

With other readers, Gray has viewed the story of cannibalism as an illustration of how far the people have been brought down. Nelson writes: 'famine robs people of their basic humanity'.[10] Reinhartz writes that 'The story illustrates the fact that the consequences of disobedience as set out in Deut. 28.56-57, the worst of which is maternal cannibalism, have indeed come to pass'. She also talks of 'cannibalism of the worst possible sort' and the 'disturbing inhumanity of the mother'.[11] These sorts of statements, which are particularly interesting coming from a collection of feminist essays, seem to be placing a special responsibility upon the mother. These statements reinforce the ideal that mothers will sacrifice themselves utterly for their children. Where is the father in all this? Why should maternal cannibalism be worse than paternal cannibalism? While it is hoped by all children that their mother will protect them from evil, it is not her responsibility alone. Who else is responsible here?

2 Kings is part of the Deuteronomistic history. This history is characterized by a number of interests: a concern with the monarchy

8.   Long, *2 Kings*, p. 92; Lasine, 'Jehoram', p. 27.
9.   John Gray, *I and II Kings* (OTL; London: SCM Press, 1964), p. 523.
10.   Richard Nelson, *First and Second Kings* (Interpretation; Atlanta: John Knox Press, 1987), p. 189.
11.   Adele Reinhartz, 'Anonymous Women and the Collapse of the Monarchy: A Study in Narrative Technique', in Athalya Brenner (ed.), *A Feminist Companion to Samuel and Kings* (The Feminist Companion to the Bible, 5; Sheffield: Sheffield Academic Press, 1994), pp. 43-65 (55).

(which often seems ambivalent); the centralization of the cult; an interest in false and true prophecy;[12] the belief that when Israel was obedient and faithful to God it would receive blessings but if it 'walked after other gods' it would bear the results of curses.[13] This last concern casts light on the context of the famine and cannibalism. As Reinhartz has pointed out, Deut. 28.53-57 presents cannibalism as one of the curses for covenantal disobedience. The one who delivers the curse is God (Deut. 28.48, 59).

Lasine's article (mentioned above, n. 1) raises some interesting and important issues. He sees the cannibal mothers as symbolic of the world upside down. Mothers who eat their children are not what one would expect. He points out that the prophets Isaiah and Micah use cannibal imagery to describe social turmoil (Isa. 9.18-19; Mic. 3.3). He refutes LaBarbera's arguments that the text is 'a cleverly constructed satire on the ruling elite of the day'.[14] The king is drawn in a sympathetic light. Despite the fact that he does not appear to respond directly to the woman, he 'registers the horror of the inverted world by making an urgent, desperate judgement...the call for the death of Elisha—[which] shows that he has not lost all sense of urgent social responsibility'.[15] After reading the previous chapters the reader knows the king has been led to expect that Elisha is intimately connected to God. He can fix things. The king is wearing sackcloth which is a symbol of mourning and repentance. He appears to be conscious of his shortcomings and hopeful in God. Initially he tells the woman to look to the Lord for help, but by the time he reaches Elisha's door he has given up hope. Perhaps he too thinks God has gone too far in allowing cannibalism. The reputations of Elisha and God are at stake in this text.

In the final part of Lasine's essay he looks at the social function of the passage and the theodicy it may suggest. He suggests that a puzzling paradox is presented. It seems that the world is turned upside down and the goodness of human nature is reversed ultimately because God made it so. The key is that God has been metaphorically related to the mother who cannot forget her child (Isa. 49.15). As Lasine writes, it is clear that God can forget her children.[16] If God is

12. Nelson, *First and Second Kings*, p. 13.
13. Gray, *I and II Kings*, pp. 37-42.
14. Robert LaBarbera, 'The Man of War and the Man of God: Social Satire in 2 Kings 6.8–7.20', *CBQ* 46.4 (1984), pp. 637-51; quoted in Lasine, 'Jehoram', p. 38.
15. Lasine, 'Jehoram', pp. 39-40.
16. Lasine, 'Jehoram', p. 46.

compassionate then why have God and Elisha chosen not to react? Of course, in ch. 7 a miracle does occur and food becomes available, but it comes too late for the woman and her child. What ideology is presented here?

Lasine asks,

> Are the readers being led to condemn the king as well as the cannibal mother and to accept Elisha's passivity and God's mode of punishment? Or is the audience to affirm Jehoram's desperate response and to question Elisha's behaviour and the fairness of divine punishment, in spite of the fact that the Deuteronomistic History is generally assumed to reflect prophetic interests, to be theologically opposed to the northern kings, and to be based on a schema of divine retribution?[17]

These questions clearly sum up the issues that are put to the reader, yet I still feel uneasy. They put the reader in the shoes of God and Elisha, and then, in the king's. What they do not do is put the reader in the shoes of the woman. Standing in the woman's position there is no question of God's fairness. Elisha saved the Shunammite's son. Was her child any less worthy? He fed one hundred men. Was she any less worthy? While Lasine raises the issue of God's responsibility for cannibalism, it is the woman who bears the weight of his (and Reinhartz's) condemnation.

Lasine writes,

> Foremost of the [bizarre elements of the story] is the complainant's callousness and her utter obliviousness to the fact that she has committed an abominable crime. When she approaches the king her sole concern is with the injustice she believes she has suffered because the other woman reneged on an agreement. She states all this publicly without shame, and even acts as though she assumes the king will share her view of the situation. Retaining an absurdly narrow focus on a relatively trivial issue while ignoring a colossal problem is typical of characters in a comedy.[18]

Yet, if the famine and her cannibalism are the results of the curse of God, the mother has become a victim of circumstance at best, and God at worst. There is no suggestion that she has sinned against God as an individual; covenant-breaking is the sin of the nation. If cannibalism was as commonplace in antiquity as has been suggested, then she may not view it as a crime at all, although this is not to say that in ordinary circumstances she would not feel deep anguish.[19]

17. Lasine, 'Jehoram', p. 47.
18. Lasine, 'Jehoram', p. 28.
19. Gray, *I and II Kings*, p. 523.

But these are not ordinary circumstances. Another point raised by Lasine is the woman's complete obliviousness to her action. Having recently eaten her child this mother is now expected to show emotion! How could one possibly eat one's own child and have emotion left to express? How could one have eaten the child in the first place without having first withdrawn all sense of connection, responsibility and feelings from that child? In effect, the mother had to cease being the child's mother. To become emotional, to become the child's mother again at the point of approaching the king, would mean that she would then have to face the consequences of her action and psychologically accommodate them. To express shame would probably be the death of her. Lasine suggests the woman is focusing on a relatively trivial issue. Yet, if the mother's sanity is to be held intact, it is essential that her action is validated by the other woman giving up her son also. It is not a trivial matter.

Lasine sees comedy as a social event; it begins when the 'comic' ceases to be conscious of his fellow beings. This woman is comic because she shows no public shame.[20] He relates her indifference to that of the Levite who tells his concubine to get up when she lies murdered at the door. 'In both stories grotesque humour conveys the essence of an inverted world in which social relations have totally broken down.'[21] There is something deeply disturbing about this idea. It may well be true that some find it humorous—irony is undoubtedly present in the story—and indeed it would certainly represent a topsy-turvy world, but it remains that a woman is forced into an extraordinary action at an extraordinary time. When the social structures let her down; when king, prophet and God cease to provide, she is still expected to behave in a way with which society feels comfortable. When she does not, she becomes comic. However, it is difficult to hear her laughter.

Reading Here and Now

When I read with the cannibal mother I find a story of betrayal and powerlessness. The only person she can access is a kindly, but peculiarly powerless king. Those that hold the real influence are shut away behind closed doors. The true cannibals in this story are those spoken of in Mic. 3.3 and Isa. 9.19-20. These are the rulers of Israel who eat the flesh of God's people, and God, the Cannibal Parent, who

---

20. Lasine, 'Jehoram', p. 33.
21. Lasine, 'Jehoram', p. 39.

allows it. The most difficult aspect of the woman's experience is knowing that food was only a miracle away.

This story has a familiar ring to it, as does the response of the critics. At the time of writing (August 1997) there is a controversy in the news media surrounding a woman who killed her baby. Certainly, her position is not comparable to the cannibal mother in its extremity. Her diet, while minimal, would not have been below the level that would sustain life and she was not resident in a beseiged city. However, on the issues of access to resources, lack of control of her own circumstances and hopelessness, comparison may be warranted. While the contemporary mother's circumstances were complex and her action cannot be condoned, her situation is shared by many women raising children alone and having to rely on the state for their income. At her trial, the defence showed that she had received only a third of the financial assistance to which she was entitled from the state to raise her four children.

Regardless of exactly how much money she had to live on—even the maximum state entitlement is undoubtedly low—her position of powerlessness is notably similar to that of the cannibal mother. She is surrounded by food and resources. The representatives of the state she approaches for help are often kindly, but not always. However, they too are similarly powerless to act without the authority of the men behind closed doors (Mic. 3.3). In the language of Micah they flay her skin and break her bones. But no, she broke the bones of her baby. Who is doing the (b)eating? Those in power place the responsibility squarely upon the woman. Certainly her hand struck the final blow, but the first blow was not hers.

What can be done with a text like 2 Kgs 6.24–7.20? When it is read with the concerns of a powerless mother in mind, it is difficult to dismiss the episode as another in which Israel gets the justice it deserved as the result of covenant disobedience. Can we dismiss the influence of the story of the cannibal mother upon the judgment of the mother in Aotearoa/New Zealand, even separated so radically by time, space and culture? I think not. Obviously, the Bible, and how it has been read, is embedded in many of our cultures. I suggest that this short episode cannot be passed over as an obscure and abject textual moment without consequence. While it may not be as well known as the story of Eve and Adam, the mother's story has no less potential power to influence and adds another negative image in the cumulative picture of women in the Bible.

With biblical stories like that of the cannibal mother there is no room for complacency. While feminist criticism has been pursued for a number of decades and exciting new approaches beckon, there is still much to be read and said. We interpreters must retain an awareness of the power we have to 'revictimize' characters and/or reinforce negative images of women. Elisha and God seem irredeemable from the woman's perspective. As with much theodicy there is room for anger toward God and God's representatives. Unfortunately for the woman, she cannot step out of the story and wonder if God has been co-opted into the Deuteronomist's theology, but I am not sure that would relieve her pain.

BIBLIOGRAPHY

Al Wardi, A., *Soziologie des Nomadentums* (Neuwied: Luchterhand, 1972).

Alter, R., 'Characterization and the Art of Reticence', in Clines and Eskenazi (eds.), *Telling Queen Michal's Story*, pp. 64-73.

—'How Convention Helps us Read: The Case of the Bible's Annunciation Type-Scene', *Prooftexts* 3 (1983), pp. 115-30.

Bach, Alice, 'The Pleasure of her Text', in Brenner (ed.), *A Feminist Companion to Samuel and Kings*, pp. 106-28.

Bailey, Randall C., *David in Love and War: The Pursuit of Power in 2 Samuel 10–12* (JSOTSup, 75; Sheffield: JSOT Press, 1990).

Bal, Mieke, *Death and Dissymmetry: The Politics of Coherence in the Book of Judges* (Chicago: University of Chicago Press, 1988).

—*Lethal Love: Feminist Literary Readings of Biblical Love Stories* (Bloomington: Indiana University Press, 1987).

—*Narratology: Introduction to the Theory of Narrative* (Toronto: Toronto University Press, 1985; repr. 1992).

—'Narrative Subjectivity', in *On Story-Telling: Essays in Narratology* (Sonoma, CA: Polebridge Press, 1991), pp. 146-70.

Bar-Efrat, Shimon, *Narrative Art in the Bible* (JSOTSup, 70; Sheffield: Almond Press, 1989).

—'Some Observations on the Analysis of Structure in Biblical Narrative', *VT* 30 (1980), pp. 154-73.

Barber, E.J.W., *Prehistoric Textiles* (Princeton: Princeton University Press, 1991).

Becking, B., and M. Dijkstra (eds.), *On Reading Prophetic Texts: Gender-Specific and Related Studies in Memory of Fokkelien van Dijk-Hemmes* (Leiden: E.J. Brill, 1996).

Becking, B., *Een magisch ritueel in Jahwistisch perspectief: 2 Kon. 4.31-38* (Utrechtse Theologische Reeks, 17; Utrecht: Universiteit Utrecht, 1992).

Ben-Barak, Zafrira, 'The Legal Background to the Restoration of Michal to David', in Clines and Eskenazi (eds.), *Telling Queen Michal's Story*, pp. 74-90.

—'The Status and Right of the g*ᵉbîrâ*', in Brenner (ed.), *A Feminist Companion to Samuel and Kings*, pp. 170-85.

Bendor, S., *The Social Structure of Ancient Israel* (Jerusalem: Simor, 1996).

Bergen, W.J., 'The Prophetic Alternative: Elisha and the Israelite Monarchy', in Robert B. Coote (ed.), *Elijah and Elisha in Socioliterary Perspective* (Atlanta: Scholars Press, 1992), pp. 127-38.

Berlin, Adele, 'Characterization in Biblical Narrative: David's Wives', in Clines and Eskenazi (eds.), *Telling Queen Michal's Story*, pp. 91-93.

—*Poetics and Interpretation of Biblical Narrative* (Bible and Literature, 9; Sheffield: Almond Press, 1983).

Bible and Culture Collective, *The Postmodern Bible* (New Haven: Yale University Press, 1995).

Bird, Phyllis A., 'Images of Women in the Old Testament', in Norman A. Gottwald (ed.), *The Bible and Liberation: Political and Social Hermeneutics* (Maryknoll, NY: Orbis Books, 1983), pp. 252-88.

Black, J., and A. Green, *Gods, Demons and Symbols of Ancient Mesopotamia: An Illustrated Dictionary* (Tessa Rickards, illustrator; London: British Museum Press, 1992).

Bledstein, A., 'The Trials of Sarah', *Judaism* 30.4 (1981), pp. 411-17.

—'Was *Habbiyâ* a Healing Ritual Performed by a Woman in King David's House?', *BR* 38 (1992), pp. 15-31.

Bowker, J., *The Targums and Rabbinic Literature: An Introduction to Jewish Interpretations of Scripture* (London: Cambridge University Press, 1969).

Brenner, A., *The Intercourse of Knowledge: On Gendering Desire and 'Sexuality' in the Hebrew Bible* (Leiden: E.J. Brill, 1997).

—*The Israelite Woman: Social Role and Literary Type in Biblical Narrative* (Sheffield: Sheffield Academic Press, 2nd edn, 1994 [1985]).

Brenner, A. (ed.), *A Feminist Companion to Samuel and Kings* (The Feminist Companion to the Bible, 5; Sheffield: Sheffield Academic Press, 1994).

—*A Feminist Companion to Esther, Judith and Susanna* (The Feminist Companion to the Bible, 8; Sheffield: Sheffield Academic Press,1994).

Clines, D.J.A., and Tamara C. Eskenazi (eds.), *Telling Queen Michal's Story* (JSOTSup, 119; Sheffield: Sheffield Academic Press, 1991).

Collon, D., *First Impressions: Cylinder Seals in the Ancient Near East* (Chicago: University Press of Chicago; London: British Museum Publications, 1987).

Conquest, Robert, *The Harvest of Sorrow: Soviet Collectivization and the Terror-Famine* (London: Hutchinson, 1986).

Corbiau, S., 'Sumerian Dress Lengths as Chronological Data', *Iraq* 3 (1936), pp. 97-100.

Coxon, Peter W., 'A Note on "Bathsheba" in 2 Samuel 12.1-6', *Bib* 62 (1981), pp. 247-50.

Daalen, A.G. van, 'Vertel mij toch al het grote dat Elisa gedaan heeft', *Amsterdamse Cahiers voor Exegese en Bijbelse Theologie* 5 (1984), pp. 118-34.

Davis, A. (ed. and trans.), *The Complete Metsudah Siddur: A New Linear Prayer Book* (New York: Metsudah Publications, 1990).

Dierichs, A., *Erotik in der Kunst Griechenlands* (Mainz: P. von Zabern, 1993).

Dijk-Hemmes, F. van, *Sporen van vrouwenteksten in de Hebreeuwse Bijbel* (Utrechtse Theologische Reeks, 16; Utrecht: Universiteit Utrecht, 1992).

—'The Great Woman of Shunem and the Man of God: A Dual Interpretation of 2 Kings 4.8-37', in Brenner (ed.), *A Feminist Companion to Samuel and Kings*, pp. 218-30.

Driver, S.R., *Notes on the Hebrew Text and the Topography of the Books of Samuel* (Oxford: Clarendon Press, 1960).

Durack, Mary, *Kings in Grass Castles* (London: Constable, 1959).

Eskenazi, Tamara C., 'Michal in Hebrew Sources', in Clines and Eskenazi (eds.), *Telling Queen Michal's Story*, pp. 157-74.

Exum, J. Cheryl, *Fragmented Women: Feminist (Sub)versions of Biblical Narratives* (Valley Forge, PA: Trinity Press, 1993).

—'Murder They Wrote: Ideology and the Manipulation of Female Presence in Biblical Narrative', in Clines and Eskenazi (eds.), *Telling Queen Michal's Story*, pp. 176-98.

—'Promise and Fulfillment: Narrative Art in Judges 13', *JBL* 99 (1980), pp. 43-59.

Fabre, M.L., and A. Geuret, 'Elie et la veuve de Sarepta: Analyse sémiotique de I. Rois 17', *Sémiotique et Bible* 14 (1979), pp. 2-14.

Fewell, Danna Nolan, 'Feminist Reading of the Hebrew Bible: Affirmation, Resistance and Transformation', *JSOT* 39 (1987), pp. 77-87.

Fewell, Danna Nolan, and David M. Gunn, *Gender, Power and Promise: The Subject of the Bible's First Story* (Nashville: Abingdon Press, 1993).

Fleming, D., *The Installation of Baal's High Priestess at Emar* (Atlanta, GA: Scholars Press, 1992).

Fokkelman, J.P., *Narrative Art and Poetry in the Books of Samuel: A Full Interpretation Based on Stylistic and Structural Analyses*, I (Assen: Van Gorcum, 1981).

Fowler, Robert M., 'Reader-Response Criticism: Figuring Mark's Reader', in J.C. Anderson and S.D. Moore (eds.), *Mark and Method: New Approaches in Biblical Studies* (Minneapolis: Fortress Press, 1992), pp. 50-83.

—'Who is "The Reader" in Reader Response Criticism?', *Semeia* 31 (1985), pp. 5-26.

Fox, E., *In the Beginning: A New Rendition of the Book of Genesis* (New York: Schocken Books, 1983).

Fuchs, E., 'The Literary Characterization of Mothers and Sexual Politics in the Hebrew Bible', in A. Yarbro Collines (ed.), *Feminist Perspectives on Biblical Scholarship* (Chico, CA: Scholars Press, 1985), pp. 117-36.

Gaster, T.H., *Myth, Legend, and Custom in the Old Testament* (New York: Harper & Row, 1969).

Gerstenberger, E.S., 'Homosexualität im Alten Testament: Geschichte und Bewertungen', in Evangelische Kirche in Hessen und Nassau (eds.), *Lesben, Schwule, …Kirche: Homosexualität und kirchliches Handeln: Texte aus Kirche und Wissenschaft* (Frankfurt, 1996).

Ginzburg, L., *Legends of the Jews* (7 vols.; Philadelphia: Jewish Publication Society, 1909).

Gordon, C.H., *The Common Background of Greek and Hebrew Civilizations* (New York: W.W. Norton, 1965).

Graves, R., and R. Patai, *Hebrew Myths* (New York: Greenwich House, 1983).

Gray, J., *I and II Kings: A Commentary* (OTL; Philadelphia: Westminster Press 1964; London: SCM Press, 2nd fully revised edn, 1977).

Gressmann, H., *Die Schriften des alten Testaments* (Göttingen: Vandenhoeck & Ruprecht, 2nd edn, 1921).

Grossfeld, B., *The Targum Onqelos to Genesis: Translated with a Critical Introduction, Apparatus, and Notes* (Wilmington, DE: Michael Glazier, 1988).

Gunn, David and Danna Nolan Fewell, *Narrative Art in the Hebrew Bible* (Oxford: Oxford University Press, 1993).

Gunn, David, *The Story of King David: Genre and Interpretation* (JSOTSup, 6; Sheffield: JSOT Press, 1982).

Haag, H., and K. Elliger, *'Storet nicht die Liebe': Die Diskriminierung der Sexualität— ein Verrat an der Bibel* (Olten: Walter Verlag).

Hackett, Jo Ann, '1 and 2 Samuel', in Carol A. Newsom and Sharon H. Ringe
(eds.), *The Women's Bible Commentary* (Louisville, KY: Westminster/John
Knox Press, 1992), pp. 85-95.

Hallo, W.W., *The Exaltation of Inanna* (New Haven: Yale University Press, 1968).

Harris, R., '*Gipar*', in E. Ebeling *et al.* (eds.), *Reallexikon der Assyriologie und vorderasiatischen Archaeologie* (8 vols.; Berlin: W. de Gruyter, 1968), III, pp. 377-79.

Harrison, R.K., 'The Matriarchate and Hebrew Regal Succession', *EvQ* 29.1 (1957),
pp. 29-34.

Hentschel, G., *2 Samuel* (Die Neue Echter Bibel, Kommentar zum Alten Testament;
Würzburg: Echter Verlag, 1884).

Hoover Rentería, T., 'The Elijah/Elisha Stories: A Socio-Cultural Analysis of
Prophets and People in Ninth-Century B.C.E. Israel', in Robert B. Coote (ed.),
Elijah and Elisha in Socioliterary Perspective (Atlanta: Scholars Press, 1992),
pp. 75-126.

Horner, T., *Jonathan Loved David: Homosexuality in Biblical Times* (Philadelphia:
Westminster Press, 1978).

Irvin, D., 'The Joseph and Moses Stories as Narrative in the Light of Ancient Near
Eastern Narrative', in John H. Hayes and J. Maxwell Miller (eds.), *Israelite and
Judean History* (London: SCM Press, 1977), pp. 180-202.

Ishida, T. (ed.), *Studies in the Period of David and Solomon and Other Essays: Papers
Read at the International Symposium for Biblical Studies, Tokyo 5-7, 1979* (Winona
Lake, IN: Eisenbrauns, 1982).

—*The Loyal Dynasties in Ancient Israel: A Study on the Formation and Development of
Royal-Dynastic Ideology* (Berlin: W. de Gruyter, 1977).

Jastrow, M., *Dictionary of the Talmud Babli, Yerushalmi, Midrashic Literature and
Targumin* (2 vols.; New York: Pardes Publishing House, 1943).

Keel, O., *Das Hohelied* (ZBK–AT, 18; Zürich: TVZ, 1986).

Kilian, R., 'Die Totenerweckungen Elias und Elisas—Eine Motivwanderung?', *BZ*
10 (1966), pp. 44-56.

Klein, Lillian R., 'Honor and Shame in Esther', in Brenner (ed.), *A Feminist
Companion to Esther, Judith and Susanna*, pp. 149-75.

—*The Triumph of Irony in the Book of Judges* (JSOTSup, 68; Sheffield: JSOT Press,
1989).

LaBarbera, Robert, 'The Man of War and the Man of God: Social Satire in 2 Kings
6.8–7.20', *CBQ* 46.4 (1984), pp. 637-51.

Lange, K., and M. Hirmer, *Ägypten—Architektur, Plastik, Malerei in drei Jahrtausenden* (Munich, 1967).

Lasine, Stuart, 'Jehoram and the Cannibal Mothers', *JSOT* 50 (1991), pp. 27-53.

Lemaire, A., 'Name of Israel's Last King Surfaces in a Private Collection', *BAR* 21.6
(1995), pp. 48-52.

Levenson, Jon D., and Baruch Halpern, 'The Political Import of David's Marriages',
JBL 99.4 (1980), pp. 507-18.

Long, B.O., 'A Figure at the Gate: Readers, Reading, and Biblical Theologians', in
G.M. Tucker *et al.* (eds.), *Canon, Theology and Old Testament Interpretation*
(Philadelphia: Fortress Press, 1988), pp. 166-86.

Long, Burke O., *2 Kings* (FOTL, 10; Grand Rapids: Eerdmans, 1991).

Matthews, D.M., *Principles of Composition in Near Eastern Glyptic of the Later Second
Millennium B.C.* (Göttingen: Vandenhoeck & Ruprecht, 1990).

Mazar, B. (ed.), *Views of the Biblical World* (4 vols.; Jerusalem: International Publishing Company, 1959).
McCarter, P.K., *Samuel* (2 vols.; AB, 9; Garden City, NY: Doubleday, 1984).
McKay, H.A., 'Gendering the Discourse of Display in the Hebrew Bible', in B. Becking and M. Dijkstra (eds.), *Gender-Specific and Related Studies in Memory of Fokkelien van Dijk-Hemmes* (Leiden: E.J. Brill, 1996), pp. 169-99.
McNamara, M., *Targum Neofiti 1: Genesis: Translated, with Apparatus and Notes* (Collegeville, MN: Liturgical Press, 1992).
Milgrom, J., *Leviticus 1–16* (AB, 3; Garden City, NY: Doubleday, 1991).
Miscall, Peter D., 'Michal and her Sisters', in Clines and Eskenazi (eds.), *Telling Queen Michal's Story*, pp. 246-60.
Miscall, Peter, *1 Samuel: A Literary Reading* (Bloomington: Indiana University Press, 1986).
Moi, T., *Sexual/Textual Politics: Feminist Literary Theory* (London: Routledge, 1985).
Moussa, A.M., and H. Altenmuller, *Das Grab des Nianchchnum und Chnumhotep* (Mainz, 1977).
Müllner, I., *Gewalt im Hause Davids: Die Erzählung von Tamar und Amnon (2 Sam 13,1-22* (HSB, 13; Freiburg: Herder, 1997).
Nelson, Richard, *First and Second Kings* (Interpretation; Louisville: John Knox Press, 1987).
Oppenheim, A. Leo, 'The Golden Garments of the Gods', *JNES* 8 (1949), pp. 172-93.
Otwell, John, *And Sarah Laughed: The Status of Woman in the Old Testament* (Philadelphia: Westminster Press, 1977).
Parrot, A., *Sumer* (Paris: Gallimard; repr. 1981).
—*The Arts of Assyria* (New York: Golden Press, 1961).
Payne, B., *The History of Costume: From the Ancient Egyptians to the Twentieth Century* (New York: Harper and Row, 1965).
Plate, S. Brent and E.M. Rodríguez Mangual, 'The Gift that Stops Giving: Hélène Cixous's "Gift" and the Shunammite Woman', *BibInt* 7.2 (1999), pp. 113-32.
Pope, M., *Song of Songs* (AB, 7c; Garden City, NY: Doubleday, 1977).
Reinhartz, Adele, 'Anonymous Women and the Collapse of the Monarchy: A Study in Narrative Technique', in Brenner (ed.), *A Feminist Companion to Samuel and Kings*, pp. 43-65.
Robinson, J., *The First Book of Kings* (Cambridge: Cambridge University Press, 1972).
Rösel, H.N., *Von Josua bis Jojachin: Untersuchungen zu den deuteronomistischen Geschichtsbüchern im Alten Testament* (VTSup, 75; Leiden: E.J. Brill, 1999).
Salisbury, Harrison E., *The Siege of Leningrad* (London: Secker & Warburg, 1969).
Sarna, N., *Genesis* (Jewish Publication Society Torah Commentary; Philadelphia: Jerusalem: The Jewish Publication Society, 1989).
Schottroff, W., 'Gleichgeschechtliche Liebe', in L. Schottroff and W. Schottroff, *Die Macht der Auferstehung: Sozialgeschichtliche Bibelauslegungen* (Munich: Chr. Kaiser Verlag, 1988), pp. 126-32.
Schweickart, P., 'Reading Ourselves: Toward a Feminist Theory of Reading', in E.A. Flynn and P. Schweickart (eds.), *Gender and Reading: Essays on Readers, Texts and Contexts* (Baltimore: The Johns Hopkins University Press, 1986), pp. 31-62.
Siebert-Hommes, J., *Let the Daughters Live! The Literary Architecture of Exodus 1–2 as a Key for Interpretation* (Leiden: E.J. Brill, 1998).

Bibliography 143

Siems, A.K. (ed.), *Sexualität und Erotik in der Antike* (Wdf, 605; Darmstadt: Wissenschaftliche Buchgesellschaft, 1988).
Sjöberg, A., and E. Bergmann, 'The Collection of the Sumerian Temple Hymns', *TCS* (5 vols.; Locust Valley, NY: J.J. Augustin, 1969), III, pp. 5-154.
Smelik, K.A.D., 'The Literary Function of 1 Kgs 17,8-24', in C. Brekelmans and J. Lust (eds.), *Pentateuchal and Deuteronomistic Studies* (Leuven: Peeters, 1990), pp. 239-43.
Speiser, E.A., *Genesis* (AB, 1; Garden City, NY: Doubleday, 1964).
Sternberg, Meir, *The Poetics of Biblical Narrative: Ideological Literature and the Drama of Reading* (Bloomington: Indiana University Press, 1985).
Stoebe, H.-J., *Das zweite Buch Samuels* (KAT, 8.2; Gütersloh: Gütersloher Verlagshaus/Gerd Mohn, 1994).
Stolz, F., *Das erste und zweite Buch Samuel* (ZBK–AT, 9; Zürich: Theologischer Verlag, 1981).
Struthers Malbon, E., and J. Capel Anderson, 'Literary-Critical Methods', in E. Schüssler-Fiorenza (ed.), *Searching the Scriptures. I. A Feminist Introduction* (London: SCM Press, 1994), pp. 241-54.
Thompson, J.A., 'The Significance of the Verb Love in the David-Jonathan Narratives in 1 Samuel', *VT* 24 (1974), pp. 334-38.
Tyndale's Illustrated Bible Dictionary (3 vols.; Leicester: Inter-Varsity Press, 1980).
Ulanov, Ann Belford, *The Female Ancestors of Christ* (Boston: Shambhala, 1993).
Valler, Shulamit, 'King David and "His" Women: Biblical Stories and Talmudic Discussions', in Brenner (ed.), *A Feminist Companion to Samuel and Kings*, pp. 129-42.
Vandersleyen, C., *Das Alte Ägypten* (Berlin: Propylaen Verlag, 1975).
Wacker, M.-T., 'Geschichtliche, hermeneutische und methodologische Grundlagen', in L. Schottroff, S. Schroer and M.-T. Wacker (eds.), *Feministische Exegese: Forschungserträge zur Bibel aus der Perspektive von Frauen* (Darmstadt: Wissenschaftliche Buchgesellschaft, 1995), pp. 3-79.
Weadock, P.N., 'The *Giparu* at Ur', *Iraq* 37 (1975), pp. 101-28.
Weizer, J., *Von anderen Ufer: Schwule fordern Heimat in der Kirche* (Düsseldorf, 1995).
Westermann, C., *Genesis* (Grand Rapids, MI: Eerdmans, 1987).
Whybray, R.N., *The Succession Narrative: A Study of II Samuel 9.2 and 1 Kings 1 and 2* (SBT, 2.9; London: SCM Press, 1968).
Williams, James G., *Women Recounted: Narrative Thinking and the God of Israel* (Sheffield: Almond Press, 1982).
Woolley, C.L., *Ur of the Chaldees* (revised by P. Moorey; Ithaca, NY: Cornell University Press, 1982).
Würthwein, E., *Die Bücher der Könige: 1. Könige 17–2. Könige 25* (ATD, 11.2; Göttingen: Vandenhoeck & Ruprecht, 1984).
Yadin, Y., *The Art of Warfare in Biblical Lands, in the Light of Archaeological Study* (2 vols.; New York: McGraw Hill, 1963).
Yee, Gail, 'Fraught with Background: Literary Ambiguity in II Samuel 11', *Int* 42 (1988), pp. 240-53.

INDEXES

INDEX OF REFERENCES

BIBLE

INDEX OF AUTHORS

FEMINIST THEOLOGY TITLES

Individual Titles in Feminist Theology

Linda Hogan, *From Women's Experience to Feminist Theology*

Lisa Isherwood and Dorothea McEwan (eds.), *An A–Z of Feminist Theology*

Lisa Isherwood and Dorothea McEwan, *Introducing Feminist Theology*

Kathleen O'Grady, Ann L. Gilroy and Janette Patricia Gray (eds.), *Bodies, Lives, Voices: Gender in Theology*

Melissa Raphael, *Thealogy and Embodiment: The Post-Patriarchal Reconstruction of Female Sacrality*

Deborah Sawyer and Diane Collier (eds.), *Is There a Future for Feminist Theology?*

Introductions in Feminist Theology

Rosemary Ruether, *Introducing Redemption in Christian Feminism*

Lisa Isherwood and Elizabeth Stuart, *Introducing Body Theology*

Melissa Raphael, *Introducing Thealogy: Discourse on the Goddess*

Pui-lan Kwok, *Introducing Asian Feminist Theology*

Feminist Companion to the Bible (1st Series)

Athalya Brenner (ed.), *A Feminist Companion to the Song of Songs*

Athalya Brenner (ed.), *A Feminist Companion to Genesis*

Athalya Brenner (ed.), *A Feminist Companion to Ruth*

Athalya Brenner (ed.), *A Feminist Companion to Judges*

Athalya Brenner (ed.), *A Feminist Companion to Samuel–Kings*

Athalya Brenner (ed.), *A Feminist Companion to Exodus–Deuteronomy*

Athalya Brenner (ed.), *A Feminist Companion to Esther, Judith and Susanna*

Athalya Brenner (ed.), *A Feminist Companion to the Latter Prophets*

Athalya Brenner (ed.), *A Feminist Companion to the Wisdom Literature*

Athalya Brenner (ed.), *A Feminist Companion to the Hebrew Bible in the New Testament*

Athalya Brenner and Carole Fontaine (eds.), *A Feminist Companion to Reading the Bible: Approaches, Methods and Strategies*

Feminist Companion to the Bible (2nd Series)

Athalya Brenner and Carole Fontaine (eds.), *Wisdom and Psalms*

Athalya Brenner (ed.), *Genesis*

Athalya Brenner (ed.), *Judges*

Athalya Brenner (ed.), *Ruth and Esther*

Athalya Brenner (ed.), *Samuel and Kings*